Orlando Saer has provided  manual for small group m biblical vision, this book i practical advice, peppered .... anecdotes and the wisdom of experience. Covering everything from who should lead to how they should lead and what they should aim for, I have great hopes for its positive impact in churches of all types and sizes. As someone with responsibility for small groups, I know this will come in very useful and so commend it warmly.

Mark Meynell
Director of Fellowship Groups,
Senior Associate Minister, All Souls Church, London

A really helpful practical guide to small group leadership which is simultaneously 'how-to' and 'can-do'.

Julian Hardyman
Senior Pastor, Eden Baptist Church, Cambridge

One of the strengths of our church life is to have small groups of Christians meeting together for study of the Scriptures and mutual encouragement and care. Orlando Saer is a shrewd, capable and experienced guide and gives practical and down-to-earth advice. He has provided us with a resource well worth study and action.

Peter Jensen
Retired Archbishop of Sydney, Sydney, Australia

Orlando Saer's *Iron Sharpens Iron* may well become the 'Bible' for small group studies – as the author's six finely wrought chapters cover virtually everything essential to initiating and maintaining healthy small group Bible studies. There is nothing arm-chair here. No bromides. Saer writes from ground-level, providing us with hard-won advice that is unexceptionably biblical, intensely practical and ever- so- wise. One could wish nothing better for small group ministries than that well-worn copies of this superb book were in the hands of all who aspire to lead. It is terrific, truly the best book of its kind I have read.

R. Kent Hughes,
Senior Pastor Emeritus, College Church, Wheaton, Illinois

This is an outstanding book full of carefully applied theological reflection and valuable practical wisdom. It will be of immense benefit to small group Bible study leaders. I recommend it wholeheartedly.

William Taylor,
Minister, St Helens Bishopsgate, London

An extremely helpful and practical guide from someone who really understands small group ministry – we shall be giving all our small group leaders a copy as soon as we can get hold of them!

Richard Coekin,
Senior Minister, the Co-Mission Initiative,
Chairman of Christian Conventions, London

Iron
Sharpens
Iron

*Leading Bible-Oriented
Small Groups that Thrive*

ORLANDO SAER

CHRISTIAN
FOCUS

Copyright © Orlando Saer 2010

ISBN 978-1-84550-575-2

Published in 2010,
reprinted 2011 (twice) and 2015
by
Christian Focus Publications Ltd.,
Geanies House, Fearn, Ross-shire,
IV20 1TW, Scotland, Great Britain.

Cover design by Paul Lewis

Printed by
Bell and Bain, Glasgow

Contents

Acknowledgments

Twenty years ago I was thrown into the deep end. 'Orlando, you can lead a Bible-study group, can't you?' asked my Christian Union leader. It was framed as a question, but he didn't wait for a response. 'Thought so. That settles it. You and John can take one on.' And so we did – in a fashion! The truth is, though, that I had never even been a member of a Bible-study group, let alone led one! Like many before and since, I had to learn on the job. Twenty years later, I'm still feeling my way.

I've had help, though. Over that time, I've read books on the subject, listened in on talks and seminars, browsed articles, discussed with experienced leaders – anything that would help me do a better job. All kinds of nuggets from all these sources have lodged themselves inside me; I dare not attempt to unpick the knot of different influences. I am unashamed to stand on the shoulders of others in this way and to acknowledge my indebtedness in this general way. That disclaimer aside, I've listed a few of the books I've found particularly helpful in Appendix 3. You might like to dig out one or two of them if you want to explore deeper.

The contents of this book began their life in a series of training seminars I gave to the 'Knowing God' leaders at Dundonald Church in Wimbledon almost 10 years ago. I'm grateful to Richard Coekin, Senior Pastor of that church and of the Co-mission network, for allowing me the time to put the work in; and to my fellow leaders of Cranleigh Baptist Church for the time to expand these to their present form more recently. Each time I've presented the material – or parts of it – the questions and comments 'from the floor' have stimulated me to expand on specific areas – particularly the contributions of delegates at a South East Gospel Partnership training day I was invited to lead four years ago. I have also had good steers along the way from some who have been kind enough to read through the text as a whole, notably Emma Hunter Dunn, Mike Gilbart Smith and Joy Horn. Their contributions have been invaluable.

Inevitably I must also thank my wife Libby. Not only has she contributed from her own experience of leading women's Bible-study groups, passed helpful material in my direction and made any number of suggestions along the way for areas which needed work; she has also uncomplainingly borne the brunt of my occasional periods of 'hibernation' as I've disappeared into my study or further afield to Oak Hill College library or Waverley Abbey, in search of the sustained peace and quiet needed for tapping out the text that follows.

Thank you all. And most of all thank you, my great God. May this book serve in some tiny way to increase the knowledge of your Word, and thereby of your Son and my precious Saviour, the Lord Jesus Christ.

OS

June 2010

1

Why Small Group Bible Study?

Small is beautiful. That is one of the maxims of the moment in Western Christianity. Recent years have seen a significant reaction against the mega-church culture in favour of smaller, more 'authentic', Christian communities. Quality of relationships has once again become more important than sheer quantity. Genuine believers want to be participants, not just consumers. They want to experience what it is really like to live out their Christian lives in the context of a group of fellow believers with whom they can share at a deep level.

It is hardly surprising that against this backdrop, Christian small groups have proliferated. Call them what you will – 'home groups', 'fellowship groups', 'ladies' groups', 'men's groups', 'discipleship groups', 'growth groups', 'cells', 'Bible study groups', or simply 'small groups' – they have become integral to the programmes of most Bible-believing churches of any size and indeed to many para-church organisations too.

But is this a good thing? Christians love to study the Bible. We're convinced that when we do, we hear God himself addressing us. But we already find ourselves opening it up in all sorts of contexts as it is: on our own, at prayer meetings of various kinds, in Sunday meetings, sometimes even at huge conventions. We're always at it! So why add yet another forum for Bible study?

Potential Pitfalls of Small Group Bible Study

Any good and worthwhile activity – from snowboarding to crossword-solving – carries with it hazards as well as its pleasures. And small group Bible study is no exception. Most Christians who have been involved in Bible study groups for a while will have their fair share of horror stories to tell. Etched on their memories are recollections of times when it all went terribly wrong. Experience has left them painfully aware of some of the potential pitfalls and drawbacks of these kinds of meetings.

So before we look at the positives, it's worth being realistic about some of the more common dangers.

The vertical is pushed out by the horizontal

If the runaway success of social networking websites teaches us anything, it is that all of us need to have a community where we feel we belong. The technology may change, but the principle does not. The need to relate is written into our DNA.

In any sizeable church, there is a tendency for the small group to become the primary 'place of belonging' or 'social unit' for the average member. And it is not hard to see why. You look around at a Sunday meeting and – unless you're a particularly gregarious sort – you feel swamped, even intimidated, by the sheer numbers of people all around. So where do you go if you want to get to know people? If you're anything like the typical church member, you retreat to the more manageable arena of the mid-week, small group meeting. That seems like the right place to develop real, meaningful friendships. And so, quite naturally, over time your fellow group members become those with whom you want to share your life most intimately. Week by week you look forward to the meeting for exactly that reason.

And why not? This dynamic is not only inevitable; it is quite natural and healthy. As we shall see later, we all need an environment where we can encourage one another personally and perhaps even become accountable to each other in some measure.

However, there is always the danger that the desire of group members to grow in relationships with one another will come to *dominate* the agenda of the group. It may not happen straight away, but like the proverbial frog in the saucepan, by the time anybody realises what is happening, the original 'culture' of the group has died. The group's social agenda has squeezed out what was most likely the group's primary purpose at the outset – to encounter God himself and to get to know him better by studying his Word together.

What has happened? The whole reason for meeting has been upturned. The group has become a social club. The 'horizontal' is all but enthroned. The 'vertical' is all but forgotten.

The message is sidelined by the method
Some years ago, I used to commute to work across the spectacular Dartmoor National Park in South West

England. I loved that trip. As you can imagine, the route was at least as thrilling as the destination!

Bible study can be just like that. The destination – discovering what God is saying right now – properly remains the focus. But the route by which we travel to that destination can be a wonderful adventure. Generation after generation of Christians has been thrilled by the process of taking the 'raw material' of words on a page and – under God's direction – reading, discussing, sharpening, refining, conceptualising and applying those words to their daily lives.

You might be able to identify with this. You know what it feels like. You are not being addressed from an unanswerable pulpit fifty metres away; you are engaged in a lively discussion with friends a mere coffee table's length away. You are not simply *allowed* to think for yourself; you are positively *encouraged* to. You are discovering biblical truth for yourself. And – on a good day – it can be nothing short of exhilarating.

But you might, just *might*, be playing with fire. The risk is that small group members become so addicted to the process itself that over time they find themselves turning their noses up at less 'exciting' forms of Bible study, such as the Sunday sermon or personal study. What has happened is that they have become addicts to the *method* of Bible study. The *message* – which ought to be, and perhaps once was, the focus – has been pushed into second place.

The blind are led by the blind
Right across history battles have been won or lost again and again, ultimately by the calibre of the general

in command. The one calling the shots is the key to a successful campaign. A wise foot-soldier would always want to serve under a great leader.

The same principle holds true in the battle for a good Bible study. One of the greatest frustrations of small group Bible study is simply poor leadership. It is probably the most common complaint voiced by group members. Discussion, they say, is allowed to drift aimlessly. Conflicting 'truths' are accepted without any attempt at resolving them. Conclusions are drawn more on the basis of the force with which the ideas were suggested or a general democratic consensus than from a rigorous examination of the text. To be sure, nobody has been offended by their ideas being rejected. But, as likely as not, nobody has made much progress either. The leader has failed to lead; the members leave having failed to learn.

Sometimes this exasperating experience comes down to mere force of circumstance. In the student world, for example, studies are often led by peers who may be both inexperienced and inadequately trained. Such leaders understandably find it unnatural and stilted to put on the leader's 'hat'. Sometimes it is justified by theological principle. 'The spirit will lead us into all truth', say the advocates of this style of meeting. 'We don't need any other kind of leader. A discussion-facilitator, perhaps, but not a leader.' Either way, whether the cause is situational or ideological, the result is simply painful. It feels to the members as though the blind are being led by the blind.

1. The vertical pushed out by the horizontal: they can turn into little more than social groups.

2. The message sidelined by the method: members can become addicts to one way of encountering God.

3. The blind led by the blind: meetings can become simply opportunities to pool ignorance.

Benefits of Small Group Bible Study

With hazards like these abounding, then, is it perhaps time to draw stumps on small group Bible study? Is the format something to shy away from? Should such groups be disbanded in order to refocus solely on the Sunday congregational meeting? Not at all! Because the benefits of the format vastly outweigh these dangers.

Let me be clear on one point here. Despite what is suggested in almost every book on small groups I have ever read, there is nothing in the Bible to say that a church *ought to* have an organised network of small groups. Or that without dividing up into such groups a church will *necessarily* be unhealthy in some way. The basic 'unit' of the church is the church itself, not some subdivision of it. But that said, small groups can be a very helpful *means* of achieving ends which certainly are demanded by the Bible of Christian churches. The New Testament abounds with instructions to Christian believers to do things to 'one another'. For example, we are to teach and admonish one another (Col. 3:16), to pray for one another (Eph. 6:18), to carry each other's burdens (Gal. 6:2) and to work with one another in evangelism (literally 'with one mind striving together for the faith of the gospel', Phil. 1:27 κjv).

How can small groups help us to take instructions like these seriously?

A good place to listen to God

My wife and I had an unusual engagement: we spent it 7,000 miles apart! There was no access to any telephone communication to speak of. So if I wanted to get to know her better, all I could do was read and re-read her letters. There would come a point when I would see her face-to-face, and I could dispense with the letter-reading. But in the meantime, that written material was what I had to get to know her better and grow in my relationship with her. And believe me, I treasured those words!

One day every Christian believer will encounter God face-to-face. But in the meantime we have the great work of his Spirit, the Bible. So interacting with God's Word is at the heart of all authentic Christian spirituality. It is in the Bible that God speaks to us personally and powerfully: 'Your Word is a lamp to my feet', wrote the Psalmist, 'and a light to my path (Ps. 119:105 εsv). Christian experience without God's Word is like a car without an engine: it might look good but it is not going anywhere anytime soon! This being so, every believer needs to make sure he or she is reading the Bible *properly*. It is important to get it right. Small group Bible study is a great way to do exactly that.

For a start, this kind of meeting is an excellent place to learn good habits (and correct bad habits) of reading the Bible – habits which will be of great use in individual study. Often young Christians have little idea about how to approach their Bible-reading in 'quiet times' or 'personal devotions'. They know it's something they're 'meant to do', yet they feel ill-equipped to do it without at least the benefit of some notes which tell them 'what it means'. Sermons can often be helpful here.

But there is always a limit to how far a preacher can show his workings. In a small group, however, this is far from the case. Methodology is always bubbling away in the background as contributions to the discussion are made, refined or corrected. And more than that, it is a natural and unthreatening environment for very basic questions on approach to be cleared up.

But it is not just a question of honing our interpretation skills. It is also about getting on and actually learning from the Bible. This is where small groups really come into their own. If you wanted to learn how to carry out basic servicing on your car, which would you choose: an hour-long lecture from a pro on 'The principles of the internal combustion engine' or an evening's practical group tutorial, getting your hands dirty down on the workshop floor? It's not a difficult choice. The interactive environment of the small group allows for extremely fruitful teaching and learning to take place; often much more so, indeed, than sitting in the pew listening to a Sunday sermon. It's a great place to 'teach and admonish one another' (Col. 3:16).

We have already seen how the primacy of the preached word on Sunday *can* sometimes be endangered by the excitement of personal discovery in the mid-week small group. The fact remains, though, that interactive communication is generally vastly more 'efficient'. The minds of group members are highly engaged and therefore receptive to information. Their particular 'wavelengths' can be reached relatively easily and content therefore appropriately packaged. Their learning can be fortified by their articulating ideas for themselves and their understanding therefore bolstered. Their specific questions can be addressed and their assumptions therefore either confirmed or corrected. Their comprehension can be questioned and their grasp of difficult concepts therefore checked. Getting your hands dirty down on the workshop floor has an awful lot going for it!

More even than this, in a small group, the door is opened to a whole variety of teaching styles. There is more than one way to skin a cat – so the saying goes. And there is certainly more than one way to convey biblical truth. This means the *way* information is communicated can be tailored to the individual group members.

It is worth pointing out that a good deal of research has been carried out in recent years about the various types of learning style favoured by different people. Some are 'visual' learners (they understand things best by *seeing* them); others are 'auditory' learners (they understand things best by *hearing* them explained); others still are 'kinaesthetic' learners (they understand things best by *doing* something). You can work out which category you fit into by thinking about your approach to different situations. When you're unsure of a spelling, do you write it out to see if it 'looks right' or say it slowly to see if it 'sounds right' or write it out to see if it 'feels right'? When you're chatting with somebody, do you prefer to meet face-to-face, to chat on the phone or to talk while doing some task together? We're all different. But in a small group, there is opportunity to adapt the *teaching* style to the preferred *learning* styles of different group members so that they can benefit the most. It is important to be deliberate about this, though; otherwise the leader is likely simply to end up teaching in the way he or she personally prefers to learn.

A good place to talk to God

Contemporary Western society has a lot to answer for! By and large, the quality and intensity of relationships we enjoy in the West today are not a patch on what many of our cousins in the developing world have.

The impact of this on churches is plain to see. In even a relatively small church, it is all too easy for individual needs – and joys – to remain unnoticed. However well-intentioned church members may be about trying to look out for their Christian brothers and sisters, keeping up to date with one another is an uphill struggle. The problem is even more acute for those in churches where members are drawn from a geographically wide area. If church members neither live nor work near each other and their only regular meeting is in the context of a large gathering, it is hard for them to be meaningfully involved in each other's lives.

This being the case, mutual prayer support is likely to be tricky, to say the least! It is hard to pray for – let alone *with* – one's fellow believers when one is largely unaware of their concerns and spends little time with them. But mutual prayer support is not optional. It is an integral part of every Christian's 'to do' list. 'Pray in the Spirit on all occasions with all kinds of prayers and requests', writes Paul, 'With this in mind, be alert and always keep on praying for all the saints' (Eph. 6:18).

A regular small group meeting does allow for significant relationships to be both developed and maintained. So it becomes a very obvious arena where we can share concerns and 'pray for one another'.

But it is not just the *opportunity* to pray in an informed way that is on offer here. There is also the question of *know-how*. Most young Christians mature in their faith at least as much through example as through verbal teaching. We've already seen how this works in the area of Bible study. It is perhaps nowhere more true, though, than in the area of prayer. Good habits for both personal and public prayer are usually caught more than they are taught. In a small group, prayer can be effectively modelled by more mature Christians for the benefit of the younger Christians very simply, as shared news and information is turned into humble prayer.

There is one more useful spin-off from this kind of regular small group prayer. That is the way it allows for a steady flow of encouragements from answered prayer. As issues come up again and again, many can testify to the great spur it has given their Christian lives to see God acting in response to the prayers of the group. So as well as opportunity and know-how, a *right attitude* to prayer is constantly and subtly being fostered: a proper sense of confidence and expectancy.

A good place to care for each other

Imagine what it would be like to surf the internet if you were the only one connected to it. It would be worse than useless. In fact, it would be impossible. There would be nothing 'there'. The internet is *defined* by the connection of multiple computers. So it is with the church. The New Testament takes it for granted that church is defined by relationships. There is the fundamental relationship between the church and Christ (as, for example, a bride relates to her husband). But there are also the individual relationships between members of the church (as different parts of the body relate to other parts).

We have already noticed how small groups can play an invaluable role in fostering significant relationships between Christians. But the importance of this cannot be stressed enough in the light of the responsibility we have to care for each other and 'carry one another's burdens' (Gal. 6:2). If individuals are to be effectively pastored and discipled, it is difficult to imagine how to achieve that without a familiarity and mutual involvement such as that fostered by regular small group meetings.

Of course, the most extreme spiritual failure from which Christians naturally want to protect each other is falling away from faith altogether. Sadly, though, while a good many churches hold their front doors wide open to the world, with friendly faces beckoning in all who will come, their back doors are even wider open and stand utterly unguarded. With the kind of mobility we are used to in our society, it could be weeks before a disappearance from the Sunday meeting is even noticed, let alone acted upon. It is an awful lot harder to 'drop out' from Christian fellowship when one is part of a small group of Christians committed to each other's spiritual welfare.

But as well as *crisis-avoidance* and *damage-limitation*, small groups offer a forum for more *routine mutual care*. Christian believers find in the small group a place where others offer to bear their burdens, where joys can be shared, where encouragements can be given and received, and where understanding, wisdom and love are available in bucket-loads.

A good base from which to reach the lost

When it comes to evangelism, there are those who seem to find it a piece of cake and those who find it one of the most terrifying prospects imaginable. I think I can count the number of people I've met in the former category on the fingers of one hand. Which leaves an awful lot of us who'd sooner crawl over broken glass than open our mouths to explain to our friends how they can get right with God.

What a liberating thing it is, then, to discover that we're not on our own in the fight to bring the gospel of grace to the world. Far from it. The ambition Paul had for the Christians in Philippi was that they would be standing together, 'contending as one man for the faith of the gospel' (Phil. 1:27). The work of evangelism, in other words, is a shared task. It's an activity where we're able to be a real help to one another.

And what better comrades-in-arms than a group of Christian brothers and sisters whom you know, trust and meet with week in, week out? The small group, of course, provides plenty of opportunity to *pray* together regularly for individual opportunities to speak and to be *held to account* for the way we conduct ourselves in this crucial area of Christian discipleship. But more than that, it is a ready-made party waiting to happen! It is the experience of countless small groups over the years that occasional events, activities, meals and other social events together provide the easiest and most natural opportunities to bring unbelievers into contact with a Christian community with the gospel message on their lips.

We learn in Proverbs 27:17 a perennial truth: 'As iron sharpens iron, so one man sharpens another.' Small groups are a wonderful context for Christian believers to sharpen one another, to help one another step forward in lives of wholehearted Christian discipleship.

1. A good place to listen to God: each can help the others study the Bible.

2. A good place to talk to God: each can pray for the others in an informed way.

3. A good place to care for one another: each can carry the others' burdens

4. A good place from which to reach the lost: members can work together to advance the gospel.

2

Preparing for Leadership

Think of those leaders who have made the most profound impression on your Christian life over the years. What was it about them exactly that softened you to their influence? What do you remember most fondly about them? Was it particular things they taught you – sermons, talks, Bible studies and the like? Or was it the sort of people they were – the manner in which they communicated those things, the qualities of their life, the way they acted towards you and shared their experience with you? In the long term, most of us, if we're honest, are more deeply impacted by the latter than the former. The lives lived by the leaders in question have remained with us at least as clearly as the message they taught.

Biblical Qualifications for Leadership

When we think about our own experience in these matters, the priorities of the apostle Paul are perhaps not surprising. He knows how we tick. When he deals with the kind of credentials that must be found in candidates for leadership positions – as he does in more than one of his New Testament letters – he is almost exclusively preoccupied with two areas: *character* and *convictions*. Look at the candidate profile he lays down for elders in the Cretan church in his letter to Titus.

> An elder must be blameless, the husband of but one wife, a man whose children believe and are not open to the charge of being wild and disobedient. Since an overseer is entrusted with God's work, he must be blameless – not overbearing, not quick-tempered, not given to drunkenness, not violent, not pursuing dishonest gain. Rather he must be hospitable, one who loves what is good, who is self-controlled, upright, holy and disciplined. He must hold firmly to the trustworthy message as it has been taught, so that he can encourage others by sound doctrine and refute others who oppose it. (Titus 1:6-9)

The list is pretty comprehensive and it lays down two main types of credentials for those exercising eldership or oversight. These are the New Testament priorities when it comes to choosing somebody for a position of Christian leadership.

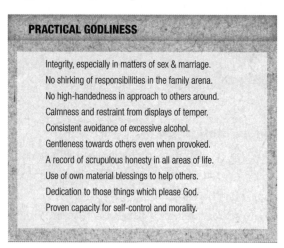

PRACTICAL GODLINESS

Integrity, especially in matters of sex & marriage.
No shirking of responsibilities in the family arena.
No high-handedness in approach to others around.
Calmness and restraint from displays of temper.
Consistent avoidance of excessive alcohol.
Gentleness towards others even when provoked.
A record of scrupulous honesty in all areas of life.
Use of own material blessings to help others.
Dedication to those things which please God.
Proven capacity for self-control and morality.

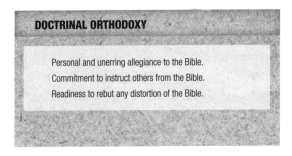

DOCTRINAL ORTHODOXY

Personal and unerring allegiance to the Bible.
Commitment to instruct others from the Bible.
Readiness to rebut any distortion of the Bible.

For those who exercise – or aspire to exercise – some form of Christian leadership (and not just church eldership), it is worth examining this checklist carefully. If I were in need of help from a neurosurgeon, I would rest easier if I knew the person fiddling about inside my head was suitably qualified for the job. Members of my small group have a right to expect at least as much of me as a leader. But there is a key difference. It is that *skills* are not at the top of the list. They are, in fact, way down the bottom. How suitable I am for Christian leadership depends *not* primarily on my skill in interpreting the Bible, how socially competent I am, my communication skills, how efficient I am in administration, my pastoral abilities, or any other such area of expertise, important as these qualities can be. Rather, scary as it may seem, it is an all-round godliness of life – allied to a passionate commitment to the teaching of the New Testament (and therefore of the Bible as a whole) – that is to mark the Christian leader.

This, of course, has great implications for the way in which one goes about the role of leading a small group. Most importantly, it means that the area which needs the hardest work is *not* relationships, programme-planning, or preparing for individual studies. It is *proactively and persistently stamping out sinful habits of living and thinking in our own lives.* Only with this ongoing commitment in place and the work of God's Spirit can leaders model the genuine Christian life. Only as they keep submitting their minds to God's word will they live and breathe sound Christian doctrine for the benefit of those they serve.

Approach to Group Leadership

It is now time to ask ourselves some tough questions. We have our 'big-picture' framework in place for the priorities of spiritual leadership. Now we need to zoom in a bit and ponder our own approach. This is where the rubber hits the road.

My first experience of being a Bible study group leader came within a few weeks of starting at university. Despite little experience of even being part of a small group, let alone leading a study, I was asked to be co-leader of one of the student Bible study groups. I had not the faintest idea what was involved. I was virtually a blank slate.

For most people, though, it's a bit different. The typical leader (and aspiring leader) will bring a whole hotch-potch of expectations, motivations and experiences to the job. And, to be quite frank, not all of them are equally worthy or helpful. So a good dose of deliberate self-criticism is an effective prescription for all who seek to lead small groups but who – when they look in the mirror – see in their own hearts an attitude or an approach that is not all that it might be.

Here are a few myths and dead-end attitudes towards the leader's role which need to be stamped on.

Brownie points with God?

One mistake is the 'spiritual brownie points' myth. This is the wrong idea that leading a small group is *a sure-fire way to improve one's relationship with God.* I described myself earlier as 'virtually a blank slate' when I started leading my first group. But even then, when I had no experience whatever of the world of small groups, the one thing I did have (even if I wouldn't have admitted it) was a vague idea that I would somehow move up in God's esteem by taking on the job. I had bought into the 'spiritual brownie points' myth.

Leadership is always a beguiling and deceptive thing. Any and all Christian leaders can very easily find themselves feeling somehow more spiritually significant than others, a bit more crucial to church life and God's plans, one step up the pecking-order, and so implicitly one step closer to God. Few would ever put it quite that way. But sadly many who exercise any kind of spiritual leadership catch themselves feeling intuitively as though they are more important or valued in God's eyes than those around.

In one limited sense, of course, this is actually right. Paul is keen that churches value 'word-gifts' (preaching, teaching and prophecy) even more highly than others. Yes, every member is crucial to the well-being of the whole body. But some roles – notably these roles to do with verbal instruction – *are* fundamental. More than that, the experience of many leaders is that leadership *has* been wonderful for their own spiritual maturity. They have found that having to teach the Bible has helped them to learn better and so understand more of

God. And having to pastor others has helped them to become less self-centred and so serve God better. In that sense, leadership can indeed foster a sense of increased closeness to God.

But – and it's a big BUT – quite the reverse can also be true. There are huge spiritual hazards involved in leadership. Any keen golfer knows the challenges involved in getting the ball from the tee to the green. There may be trees to the left, a stream to the right, a bunker before and a dip beyond. Hazards abound! And so it is with any form of Christian leadership.

The most obvious hazard is the temptation to *pride*. The flattery of being asked to serve in a leadership position and the respect the leader is given because of the office can easily lead to an unhealthly, distorted self-image. It feels like being one step further up the ladder. Pride is a widespread problem, particularly (though not exclusively!) among younger leaders.

Another danger is the temptation to *professionalism*. That is, leaders can begin to judge their own spiritual maturity by how well they perform the task in hand: the better the group is going, the more 'in tune' with God they feel. Spiritual disciplines like personal Bible-reading and prayer fade into the background as they focus attention on the more easily quantifiable tasks set before them.

To succumb to insidious temptations like these can be terribly detrimental to the leader's walk with God. It is helpful to remind oneself – and often – that each child of God stands on an equal footing in the Father's eyes: 'You are all one in Christ Jesus' (Gal. 3:28).

So the right stimulus to Christian leadership is not the desire to secure a closer relationship with God. Nothing can be done beyond what Christ has already done in achieving this. Rather, it is simply the attitude of yearning to use all that we are and all that we have to build up his church and so advance the kingdom.

Getting on to the stage?

A second wrong motivation in aspiring to small group leadership comes from viewing the role as *an effective means to increase one's standing among fellow Christians*. Every community has its elite members: the most successful, the most good-looking, the most popular, the most wealthy. In a church where the place of teaching is emphasized and the role of teachers highly valued, there is a natural temptation to seek that 'elite status' by assuming the mantle of such a leadership position.

And it doesn't stop once we are 'there', so to speak. Because then the small group leader seeks 'elite status' in the new community he or she finds herself in. Now the leader wants to be known as one of the *best* leaders – the most effective, faithful, diligent, pastorally concerned, fun and so on. The aim has become, again usually very subtly, to increase the esteem in which he or she is held in the eyes of others.

And it works! Often not quite as effectively as we thought it would, but it does work. That is what makes this particular temptation so perilous. Just as we once looked covetously at others in leadership positions, so others begin to look at us in the same way.

But this can never be a legitimate motivation for leadership. And the reason is very simple: ministry in the New Testament is not about the service of self, but about the service of Christ through the service of his people. Jesus himself both modelled as much in his own attitude and taught his followers to imitate him: 'If anyone wants to be first, he must be the very last, and the servant of all' (Mark 9:35).

So what drives the small group leader can never properly be the regard in which he or she is held by those around, but the spiritual needs of those to be served. The leader seeks above all else to pray for them, feed them and further every aspect of their spiritual maturity.

A task to be carried out?

A third misconception concerns the kind of responsibilities that are actually involved in leading a group. If ever a newly qualified schoolteacher entered the profession thinking that his or her responsibilities would begin and end with the lesson bell, it would not take many hours of a school day to end that foolish thinking!

And so it is with the small group leader. It is sometimes assumed that leadership is a matter of little more than *a one-hour-per-week task performed for a group*. There are at least three elements to this perception: the level of time-commitment; the notion of a 'task' being 'performed'; and the focus on the 'group' meeting. Each of them is wrong.

To lead a small group effectively will necessarily involve putting in *a great deal of time and effort*. The one-or two-hour meeting may be the focal point of the week and of one's relationship to the group, but it is nothing more than that. There will likely be regular meetings with other small group leaders for training, support and prayer. Diligent preparation of each study will probably take a further evening in the week – perhaps more. Forming a group identity through planning and social events and the like will take at least a further slot per term. Still more time is needed for regular prayer for each member of the group, for planning and debriefing with a co-leader, and of course personal follow-up with individuals, some of whom may be extremely demanding. It is a time-consuming business!

It should, then, be quite obvious that leading is *not primarily about a specific task to be performed.* At the very least it is a matter of a whole cluster of tasks. But it is more even than that. In truth, it is about living in a relationship with the group as teacher, nurturer, encourager, rebuker, co-disciple and – most of all – model. In that sense it is more a way of life than a quantifiable job to be done.

As to the question of focus, the focus of the small group leader must consistently remain *not so much on the group as on the individuals who comprise the group.* Working to cohere the group and foster relationships among group members is an important work in its own right: this is often the arena where the 'body life' of the church is experienced much more than in the Sunday meeting. But it must be a priority of ours to watch individuals closely in the group studies, to work hard at developing a relationship with them as individuals, and to capitalize on this by giving time to meeting with them one-to-one as often as realistically possible, in order to hold them to account in areas of practical godliness, to further their growth in spiritual maturity and to pray for and with them in an effective and informed way.

Passing on information?

One final – and related – misconception is again to do with the dynamic of the group and the leader's relationship with them. That is, there is a trend in some circles for the small group to be seen as *a forum primarily for the communication of information and imparting of knowledge.*

It is interesting to observe the way many churches promote their small groups. We have a tendency to market them as 'training courses' or 'programmes' or 'opportunities to learn more of the Bible'. That is, whether it is in order to 'sell' group membership or merely to simplify what it involves, we buy into the parlance of the adult education world and emphasize the 'intellectual' aspect of the group.

Now in some contexts, there may be a particular opportunity to use small groups to achieve an unashamed teaching and/or training goal. Indeed to some degree, the largely intellectual exercise of understanding parts of Scripture is likely to dominate the agenda of a healthy small group. And perhaps it is right that it should: according to Paul, the mind is the gateway to the person and therefore crucial to the path of Christian discipleship. However, knowledge is not an end in itself; it is a means to an end. 'Be transformed by the renewing of your mind' (Rom. 12:2) is Paul's instruction.

This has a number of implications. For one thing, the fundamental need of those we serve is not *information*; it is *transformation*. Personal transformation is our goal for every individual under our care and for every Bible study we lead.

Second, those who will benefit from our group meetings are not just the *members*, but us *leaders* too. It is the whole church which is addressed by Paul in Romans, not just the less mature. So transformation is our goal for ourselves as leaders, as well as those to whom we are seeking to minister. If the leader is genuinely sitting humbly under God's word, he or she will inevitably find areas of life addressed in the course of preparing for or leading the studies.

Third, all this only goes to emphasize the importance of *modelling godliness* as well as simply *imparting knowledge*. Once again, then, we observe the need for working at personal godliness and relationships with individuals where such modelling can take place.

Goals for Group Leadership

'Aim low', goes the saying, 'and you won't be disappointed!' If we don't have great ambitions for those under our care, there is no danger that they will fall short of our expectations.

I doubt if that is a good principle to operate by in any area of life. I am certain it is not when it comes to Christian ministry. Certainly nobody could accuse Paul of being unambitious for those he served. Look at the goal he set himself.

> We proclaim him, admonishing and teaching everyone with all wisdom, *so that we may present everyone perfect in Christ.* To this end I labour, struggling with all his energy, which so powerfully works in me.
>
> (Col. 1:28-29)

Now there is something to aspire to! It's worth pondering: what might the shape of our leadership role look like if we shared Paul's goal to present those under our care, every one of them, 'perfect in Christ'?

CHRISTIAN LEADERSHIP. . .

Leadership is for those with a proven record of practical godliness and doctrinal orthodoxy.

Leadership can be approached with wrong motivations and misconceptions.

Leadership involves setting goals for others.

3

Managing the Group

Can you remember the first time you ever went on a plane? I can. I was only 13, but I remember the experience vividly. The wide-eyed curiosity as we taxied across the tarmac, finding out all about the fascinating safety procedures. The cocktail of fear and exhilaration as the engines thundered and we left the tarmac. The sense of awe tinged with nervousness as we climbed through the clouds. The growing confidence as we levelled off at our cruising altitude and began the meal. The sinking feeling in my stomach as we started our descent. And of course the mix of anticlimax, disappointment and relief as we landed seven hours later and a whole continent away from where we started. What a buzz!

The Life Cycle of a Small Group

In some ways, being part of a small group is not so very different from the experience of sitting on that plane. It is a real journey of discovery. And every traveller on board can expect, as a direct result of being in that seat, to be hit by a whole series of emotions – positive and negative – along the way. More than that, the group itself, quite apart from the individual members, will prove to have a life of its own. It will develop its own dynamic. It will build up its own momentum. It may even come to have its own 'personality'. And in all this, through the different phases of its life, it will certainly experience its own highs and lows, quite independent of the life-experiences of its members.

So when it comes to thinking and planning for a new small group, the place to begin is not with the *activities* that the group will do together. It is with the context of those activities: the *life* of the group – its aims, culture, and values. If the group is to be effective, it is crucial that the leader steps back and lingers on these areas before diving in. Any activity that the group engages in – Bible study, prayer, mutual care, evangelism and so on – will never really 'take off' if the group remains little more than a bunch of individuals who happen to be sitting in the same room together.

I find the terminology of an aeroplane flight provides a helpful way-in to understanding the different phases in the life-cycle of a small group. If you are currently in a small group, it might be helpful to try to work out which of these phases your group is currently in. Remember, though, group life is rarely as neat or linear as the scheme – groups can regress or skip forward between the various phases.

TAXI

First of all comes *taxiing on the runway*. This is the period when all the preparations for the group's very existence are still being made. The need for a group is identified. The intended nature of the group is nailed down. Potential leaders are identified and approached. Potential members are invited and given basic information about what might be involved.

It is a time of nervous excitement, cautious optimism, perhaps non-committal inching forward step by step. Most of all it is a time of questions being raised. Who are the leaders? Who else is joining? What day do we meet? What time? When will I get home? How often? What will we do? What will we study? What level of commitment is involved? Is it really my cup of tea?

Much of what is going on in the minds of the group's members at this stage is likely to depend on (a) their feelings about the other members of the group and (b) their confidence in the leader. The leader's primary roles, then, are to ensure – usually in liaison with the small group's co-ordinator and the co-leader if there is one – that the particular 'mix' of people is likely to 'work', and to make and communicate tentative plans for the group, all the while being sensitive and flexible to the needs and circumstances of the individuals.

Issues to consider when starting a new group

1. Focus: What kind of group will it be?
Is its primary purpose to help enquirers, to train believers, or to study the Bible together and support each other?

2. Life Expectancy: Is it open-ended or fixed-life?
To stop groups getting stodgy, many small group ministries build in a 'shelf life' of maybe 1 or 2 years, after which groups are mixed up.

3. Study Programme: Who is responsible for setting it?
In our church, we find that a good balance between meeting the individual group's needs and staying together as a church is for all groups to share a study programme for two of the three terms of the year (i.e. it is set by the leadership and the small groups' co-ordinator), and for the group to set its own programme for the remaining term.

4. Personnel: Who is involved in organising the group?
You may wish to appoint a co-leader (and clarify their role), a host for the meetings, and maybe a social secretary!

5. Time and Place: What are the details for the meetings?
A home is often the obvious choice, but it could be that a church building, a hall, or even a cafe might be more suitable. The time will depend on the availability of the members.

6. Size: How big should the group be?
This is likely to depend on the size of the room where you meet. As a rule of thumb, about 8-12 often proves a good size.

7. Make-up: How diverse is the group going to be?
Since the group often provides the members' chief experience of church relationships, it may be wise to mix it up a bit (unless, for example, there is a particular training agenda and the group has a fixed life).

TAKE-OFF

Plans have been made. The group is recruited. Practicalities have been worked through. And now the day has come for *take-off* – the group's first meeting!

The atmosphere is likely to be slightly tense, even awkward. Members may be sizing one another up, looking for assumptions they have made to be confirmed or disproved, working out whether they fit in. Perhaps more than they ever will again, they will be looking to their leader to *give* a lead and take control.

The leader's key responsibilities at this first meeting, and into the next two or three meetings, are to put members at their ease, to instil an enthusiasm about the future of the group and to explain its purposes. But this is easier said than done. There will be more to say about some of the practicalities and dynamics as regards a typical group meeting when we get to chapter 5. But the following box offers a few tips to help get things off to a flying start.

Making sure the first meeting goes smoothly

1. Do your homework!
Find out as much as you possibly can about the members before the first meeting. Ideally you will have met with them and perhaps chatted to one or two people (if they have been in a group before, you could start by speaking to their previous leaders). Simply knowing that they have two other children by a previous marriage, or that they are allergic to cats, or that the only hot beverage they can stomach is elderflower tea could save all sorts of embarrassment!

2. Name names!
If people don't know one another at all, they will feel they are making progress if they can at least remember the names of those around them

---

by the end of the meeting. So you will be doing them a great service simply by making introductions at the beginning. But you can go further by (a) repeating the round of introductions every time a member arrives through the door; and (b) trying to use people's names every time you address them during the course of the evening. (If you find this feels forced, don't be embarrassed to explain exactly what you're doing and why!)

3. Cut the cringe!
If somebody feels embarrassed about even a trivial thing, that embarrassment can easily cast a dark cloud over the entire meeting. So do make a point of anticipating issues and expelling embarrassment in the way that any good host might do: explain where the toilet is, apologise for being hard to find, keep children and dogs out of the way unless you are sure everyone is comfortable with them, make sure guy-with-bad-breath is not too close to anyone else, and so on.

4. Stock up!
Eating together has always been a bonding experience and therefore an integral part of Christian community life. As the early Christians began their life together in the wake of Pentecost, we are told that they 'devoted themselves to... the breaking of bread' (Acts 2:42 – almost certainly a reference not to the Lord's Supper but simply to sharing meals). So the more food the better! (And the more effort that has obviously gone into the food, the better.) If your group meets in a home, I would suggest beginning group life – perhaps even for a few weeks – with a full meal, or at the very least some substantial dessert, though do be on the look-out for allergies and dieters!

5. Speak up!
Remember, members of the group are information-hungry at this point. They want to know all your ideas for how the group might develop, its programme, its priorities, its ground-rules, how refreshments will work, etc. – and quite possibly to contribute some ideas of their own. Encourage members to share their experiences (good and bad) of previous groups and their hopes and fears for the new group – and listen hard to what they say! Many groups have also found it helpful for the long term to spend time in their early weeks coming up with a kind of 'covenant' or joint agreement, putting into words something of the ethos they would love to see develop and are prepared to commit to. You might consider beginning to facilitate the

formation of such a covenant in the early weeks of the group's life. (See Appendix 2 for a sample small group covenant.)

CLIMB

The third stage of the group's flight-plan is *climbing* – the phase where confidence and momentum grow fast, and members begin to become more at ease with one another and their own place within the group.

People are now beginning to feel 'safe' and to know one another's boundaries, so a sense of fun and humour can now begin to be a part of the group's dynamic. They are also just beginning to move beyond the facts and are ready to start testing the water in making themselves vulnerable to one another. Prayer requests move from the factual-but-not-revealing ('Charlie's interview is on Monday') to feelings-revealing ('I'm feeling quite anxious about Charlie's interview and what I'll say if it doesn't go well').

The leader would do well to nurture this development by modelling vulnerability (e.g. entrust your personal feelings to the group), defusing awkward moments, avoiding intensity, and perhaps by encouraging a social event where members can 'hang out' in a different environment, thus producing shared history and memories for the group. You will find some ideas for such events in the box.

Ideas for group social events

The kind of events that will provide an opportunity for the group to bond will depend very much on the make-up, interests, commitments, age and mobility of the members. But here are some tried-and-tested ideas to get your creative juices flowing!

1. A walk in the country – ending at a tea-room or a pub!

2. A picnic in the park or a barbeque in someone's garden.

3. An evening out, having a go at tenpin bowling or ice-skating.

4. A trip to the cinema or a concert – followed by a meal out, or at least a drink.

5. A Christmas meal together – with everyone playing a part in the preparation.

6. Challenging another home-group to a football game or some other sporting match.

7. A weekend retreat away together in the country or at the seaside.

CRUISE

'Cruising' is a word we often use with negative overtones – perhaps with shades of complacency and comfort. But it is not in that sense that I use the word here. This phase of the group's life is the 'high point'. Everything is functioning well. A real sense of trust has developed. Members are actively engaged in one another's lives. There is a common commitment to the group as a whole. And as a result, all are prepared to work hard at coming to grips with the word of God and to pray together meaningfully. Each member is taking strides forward in his or her walk with the Lord as a result of being part of the group.

There is inevitably the occasional burst of turbulence – a discussion that turns into an argument, the occasional moment of tension as somebody takes offence at a passing comment, the odd meeting where members leave unsatisfied by where they've got to – but the group spirit proves robust enough to weather such storms. See the box below for some of the characteristics of a healthy group in the 'cruising' phase.

The challenge now for the leader is to build on this robust dynamic. Now may be the time to begin training up one or two members for a leadership role: perhaps give them a chance to lead a study or give a presentation. It may be the point to start to think seriously about taking a gospel-initiative together: maybe plan a social event to which all agree to invite a couple of friends. If the group is big, it could be an idea to start discussing the idea of subdividing and giving birth to a new group.

Characteristics of a group in good shape

1. A shared determination to grow in Christian disciple-ship, welcoming the challenges and hard work which that may entail

While enjoying each other's company, members turn up to each meeting not primarily for the social event but in order to do business with God. They are coming not for an 'uplifting' experience but to be helped – as well as to help others– in their own understanding of God's word, wanting their thoughts, feelings and behaviour to be moulded and trained by what they learn. They have done any preparatory work diligently,

---

ready for the meeting. And they come prepared to learn and grow from the model or the relationships of their fellow-believers as well as from the text of the Bible.

2. An overwhelming atmosphere of trust and respect, so fostering a genuine openness and honesty

Members have learned to respect one another and are confident in being respected by others. They know that confidences will not be betrayed either maliciously or carelessly. They know too that they won't be jumped on if they say something stupid, and that even when there are disagreements, others will seek to understand their views and the reason they hold them. They therefore contribute freely to discussion and willingly share personal information even where this may make them vulnerable. The feeling of 'safety' also means members are prepared to try out new ways of serving, so that the group functions to nurture the gifts of its members, so benefiting the wider church or Christian community.

3. A high level of participation and engagement, leading to common goals and vision for the group

Members approach meetings with a sense of anticipation and excitement, seeing attendance as not so much a chore or a commitment to be fulfilled, but as a joy. Nothing bar physical sickness, family obligations or unexpected work crisis will keep them away! There is a feeling of every member pulling their weight in the discussion, not just waiting for someone else to come up with the answer. And this spills out into the life of the group beyond the discussion. Members are more than willing to help out with refreshments or organise social events. They happily make suggestions for other activities they can be involved in together, and where their suggestion is not the one taken up by the group as a whole, they feel no resentment but quickly 'buy into' the group's plan.

4. A noticeable ethos of love and acceptance, so providing an attractive witness to Christ

Group members know that, however they are received in the wider world, in the group they can be assured of genuine, affectionate love and acceptance. They are sincerely interested in the lives of their co-members. They are patient with one another's quirks and foibles. They sincerely share in each other's joys and heartaches.

And they actively seek to help each other in practical ways during the course of their week – they help paint each other's bathrooms, cook for each other's families in times of crisis, drive each other to the airport, look after each other's kids, help each other break into their own houses when they've lost the keys! And the love they have for one another spills out in conversations with others outside the group, such that unbelievers are intrigued and find themselves strangely attracted to the warmth of this community. So when the group puts on an event of some kind, these unbelievers say 'yes' to the invitation: they really want to find out about the powerhouse behind this loving community.

DESCEND

Sooner or later, every group finds itself starting a *descent*. There may have been a particular trigger (the departure of a couple of key members, a change of leadership, an obvious rift or conflict that has been allowed to take root) or things may just have begun to lose steam. Either way, there is a sense that things are not what they were. There is a looking back to the 'glory days' with a sense of loss.

This is a difficult time for the leader, who may find accusing fingers pointing at him or her because of the apparent stalling of the group. This may or may not be fair. But it is important to keep your nerve and think clearly about the way forward.

It is rarely helpful for a leader to indulge in self-pity at his or her apparent failure to keep the group's momentum going. Far better to consult (with both the group and other wise heads) about how you as leader can serve the group best at this juncture. Look at the box for some important guidelines on what to do (and what not to do) when your group moves into this phase.

Dos and don'ts for leaders of groups in decline

<u>Don't</u> try and get things back on track by adding a new member.
   (It won't work; you'll just drag him or her down too!)

<u>Do</u> consider *changing the whole dynamic* by adding 3-4 members.
   (This is a fresh start and gets back to 'take-off'.)

<u>Don't</u> get defensive about criticism directed at you as leader.
   (You will only make things worse!)

<u>Do</u> take it on the chin, spot the kernel of truth, act and *move on*.
   (Model humility and graciousness under fire to all.)

<u>Don't</u> feel you are on your own in deciding what to do.
   (Your heavenly Father is waiting to hear your prayers!)

<u>Do</u> *liaise* with your co-leader and small groups' co-ordinator.
   (Their support, wisdom and experience will help.)

<u>Don't</u> try and hang on till the bitter end.
   (Grasping the life-cycle will minimise feelings of defeat.)

<u>Do</u> *consider closing* the group and redistributing members.
   (You might serve them better by this course of action.)

LAND

All groups *land* sooner or later. Many groups would have been far wiser to land an awful lot sooner than they do. When the time comes to close the group, the key is to avoid a crash landing (as in the diagram above!) and work instead for a smooth one.

Here are a few tips for negotiating such a landing.

Tips for negotiating a smooth landing

1. Share
Share your rationale for drawing things to a close, including the group as a whole in the decision where possible.

2. Guide
Think carefully about what you think the best thing is for each member of the group and make suggestions, but try to give genuine options.

3. Plan
If the members are to be redistributed to other groups, try to work out the timing so as to 'build in' a break for them – at the very least, a long summer holiday.

4. Rest
Leaders would be wise to take a break from leading themselves if possible. Take a sabbatical and restore your batteries!

5. Steer
Do what you can to see the members into their new groups. Speak to them about their new leader and instil confidence in them. Have a word with the new leader, passing on useful information where appropriate. And check how things are going a couple of times in the early weeks of their transition.

4

Mapping Out the Study

In 1911, one of the most exciting finds of modern times was made in the dense jungle of eastern Peru. For centuries, archaeologists with an interest in Latin America had been fascinated by the location of the 'lost city of the Incas', about which rumours had circulated since the time of the Spanish invasion. But in that year, a Yale academic by the name of Hiram Bingham set off with a field team in tow in search of this famous site. They had quite an adventure! They beat through dense jungle, questioned uncooperative locals and risked their lives on near-vertical slopes. But eventually Hiram Bingham and his team made the discovery of a life-time. In what must be one of the most inaccessible spots on earth, and almost completely buried in the vegetation, he discovered an entire city that had been lost to the world. It had been worth all the blood, sweat and tears! Almost immediately, a trail through the undergrowth was made, then a railway. And now, in the wake of that initial discovery, tourists from all over the world have been able to experience for themselves the sight of Macchu Picchu.

When you lead a Bible study, your great desire for the group is that they might be able to discover hidden treasure. You have the humbling privilege of being their guide to the life-changing experience of encountering God himself! But before you can put on your guide's 'hat' and help others make that great discovery, you need to make it for yourself and then beat back the bushes to prepare a trail for them. Before you do that, you are in no position to help anybody.

So what follows in this chapter is a summary of the key steps involved in preparing a Bible study.

Study the Text

It may be your habit as a small group leader to make use of some of the many published Bible study guides that are available. Or perhaps your small groups' co-ordinator produces questions and notes for you. These can certainly be very useful for getting you going and giving ideas for ways to approach the passage. But if you are to serve your group well, you will need at the very least to *adapt* such material, and realistically it is usually best to start at the very beginning in your own study of the text in order to lead the study most effectively. So what follows is a brief introduction to some of the basic principles of good Bible study.

Good Bible study is a bit like what the detective does in a good old-fashioned murder mystery! There are always three vital phases involved in his work. He begins with *observation*. We watch Poirot find out all he can from witnesses, clues, the autopsy, interviews, potential motives and the like. He listens, watches, smells and generally uses his imagination to make himself sensitive to all the data available to him. Then comes *interpretation*. This is the fun part. Little by little Poirot pieces all the clues together with 'ze little grey cells' to identify suspects and develop theories about what really happened. It is a slow and painstaking process, often a matter of 'three steps forward and two back'. But he always gets there in the end. Finally comes *application*. Here is the classic 'library scene' or similar dramatic dénouement. Having put all the pieces of the jigsaw together, he is in a position to take action and see through the actual arrest. With that, his work is done.

Translated into Bible study terms, this means three key stages:

1.   What does it say?
2.   What does it mean?
3.   What does it mean for me?

Observation: What does it say?

The first stage is *observation*. This is the task of working out simply what the text actually says. That might seem obvious enough: the words are there on the page in black and white! We are concerned at this stage, however, not just with the words themselves (though sometimes they may indeed present a significant challenge) but with the connection between them and the points that are being made by the author.

Observation begins, naturally enough, with *reading*. Again, this may seem obvious, but it is impossible to stress the importance of not bypassing this crucial step. Read the passage, not once, but several times.

- Read *prayerfully* (because it is the work of the Spirit who inspired the words to make them clear to us)

- Read *reflectively* (because the way the Spirit does make them clear is through our mental faculties)

- Read *inquisitively* (because it is only by interacting with the text that we can rid ourselves of sloppy assumptions about what we *think* the text is saying).

After immersing yourself in the passage in this way, the time will come to be more active in your analysis of it. Remember, there is nothing 'unspiritual' about this analytical approach: God has chosen to reveal himself and his purposes in human language – words and phrases in sentences with grammar and syntax – which means we need to muster all the basic comprehension skills at our disposal to make sure we hear God clearly. To do this well, many find it helpful to type up the text (or download it from http://bible.gospelcom.net) and print it out, perhaps double-spaced to allow for scribblings!

Good analysis begins with *division*. Try to divide up the passage into sections or paragraphs based largely on the subject matter (but taking into account other factors such as 'tone' or writing style or mood). At this stage your judgements are likely to be largely intuitive. So you may be unsure about the exact divisions; you might come up with several schemes or breakdowns. Once you have identified the sections, have a go at summarising the content of each one. You should end up with a list of the main points communicated in the passage.

This is all, of course, 'preliminary': these points will have to be revised in due course. But at least you have something to work with. Now is the time to start diving into the nitty-gritty of the text. Look through each section for repeated words or ideas. Note down any key characters or events that seem to be in the author's mind. Highlight any quotations from other parts of the Bible that seem to have some bearing on what is being said. All these things are giveaway signs for how the author's mind is working and how the passage is constructed.

You are now in a position to ask even more *questions* of the text. Don't be afraid of the simple ones – they are often the most fruitful in our Bible study. For example, Who's writing (or speaking)? To whom? What is he trying to show? Why does he record this event or use that expression? Why does he include it at this point? How does he argue it? What does that word mean? And so on.

It's important too to be clear on the *intended effect* of the passage. What impact is the writer trying to have on the reader? Sometimes, it may be a case of simple *instruction*. We are being taught truths and concepts through explanations and arguments. Other times it is more a matter of *exhortation*. We are being told how to behave in response to those truths. Still other times it is a matter of *illustration*. We are being told a story so that we can identify with particular characters and have the point of the story impressed on our minds in a different way to straightforward point-by-point teaching.

Finally, it is helpful to have a good look at the *flow* of the passage. Look carefully at the logic, that is, the way the sentences and ideas are connected. Clues to this may be found in the connecting words used (e.g. 'but', 'therefore', 'since', 'so that', 'however', 'so then', etc.). Watch out however, some Bible translations cut out some of these words, so it might be worth having a more 'literal' translation on hand. From time to time (especially in the letters of Paul!) the logic is so complicated that we need to draw up a kind of 'flow diagram' in order to work out how the argument holds together. But it is crucial to be clear on the logic: the connection between the points is often as important as the points themselves.

With all this work done, you can now go back to your original draft breakdown of the passage and revise it. Again we are interested primarily in two things: the chief divisions in the passage and the major points being made in each of those sections.

Interpretation: What does it mean?

If the goal of the 'observation' stage was to find out what the text says, the aim in this next phase of our study is *what the text means*. There may, of course, be some considerable overlap in these two steps. The dividing line is a bit blurred. But the intention now is to discern the principles that emerge from the text and which are therefore of great importance to the twenty-first-century reader. You will inevitably have to move outside the passage itself and even outside the book to determine this.

Your first task here is to work out something of the context of the passage we are studying. In other words, where does it fit into the structure of the book (i.e. the argument in the case of a Pauline letter; the narrative or plot in the case of a gospel or Acts, etc.). Indeed the book may have very obvious subdivisions. In which case, you need to be clear too on where the passage fits within that subdividision. And more specifically still, you need to bear in mind the relationship between the passage and the immediately preceding one: there may be direct or indirect allusions to it or assumptions which come from it which determine what the passage is talking about.

Moving further back, it is worth asking the question, if you have not done so already, what kind of literature am I dealing with here? A number of different literary genres are to be found in the Bible. There is history-writing (e.g. 1–2 Kings), poetry (e.g. the Psalms), straightforward narrative (e.g. Genesis), apocalyptic (e.g. Revelation), rhetoric (e.g. the speeches in Acts), gospel (e.g. Luke), propositional argument (e.g. Romans) and so on. The kind of literature you are dealing with has a direct bearing on the way you will approach it: you wouldn't, for example, expect in the Psalms the same logical rigour and precision as you find in Paul.

Now it's time to go still further back to discover how the passage fits into the context of the whole Bible. Because the whole Bible is inspired by the same author (the Holy Spirit), tells a coherent story (about the relationship between God and humanity) and is focussed on a single character (Jesus Christ), we expect to find unity throughout, from Genesis to Revelation. You therefore need to know what points of the Bible's doctrine are relevant to or taught by your passage. Clearly if, on a superficial reading, the passage seems to contradict what is taught in other parts of the Bible, then you might want to take another look! More than that, the place within the 'plot' of the Bible (what theologians sometimes call 'redemption history') is going to have to be carefully considered in order that you can work out the principles which are relevant today.

It is now time to return to the passage again and rework your breakdown of its major points and lessons. At this stage, though, you can go still further and distil the content of the passage into one single, chief point; alongside other subsidiary, 'scaffolding' points. You now have a reasonable grasp of the meaning of the passage.

Application: What does it mean for me?

The final step required for the study of any Bible passage is to reflect on application, that is, not simply what the text says or means, but *what the text demands* of its readers. Any Bible student who fails to take this step is open to the charge of being merely 'cerebral' or imitating those Pharisees whom Jesus so roundly condemned. Contrary to what some Christians think, application is not all about 'doing'. There is much more to it than that.

First of all, application will involve looking for *truths that need to be believed*. This is application to the mind, where understanding turns into belief. In a sense, every passage will contain – at some level – teaching about God, about Christ and about myself. Although it may be tempting to glide quickly past these lessons, you must be careful that you do not bypass them altogether. Often, they will be the major point of the passage (especially in narrative). Beyond that, there are of course innumerable other lessons for you to learn in the Bible. You'll naturally be on the look-out for them. Remember: Christian transformation always begins with the 'renewing of your mind' (Rom. 12:2).

Second, application will involve looking for *attitudes to be fostered*. This is moving beyond information to an appropriate response of the heart. For example, a promise in the passage should be greeted by us with an attitude of trust. An exposition of God's wonderful mercy towards us may be met by an attitude of thanksgiving. An exposition of the sinfulness of the human heart ought to lead to an attitude of confession. These are all areas of our heartfelt attitudes to God (or perhaps to ourselves or those around us) which need to be shaped by what we learn.

Third, application will involve looking for *behaviour to be modified*. That is, you are now looking at application to the will. You may have come across an example of a life pleasing to God – so imitate it. You may have read a catalogue of sinful actions which displease him – so avoid them. You may have been confronted with a virtue that is commended or an instruction that is commanded – so resolve with the help of God's Spirit to reform your life accordingly.

In all this, even in the realm of 'truth to be believed', it is helpful to be 'concrete' in your thinking. You might ask: *How* can I do this in my particular situation? *When* will I do it? In *what* circumstances? *Who* will help me to do it? *How* can I foster that attitude? *Where* will it show itself? And so on.

Finally, three caveats:

- **Look in the mirror!**

Take good care to apply the passage to yourself before applying it to others. Quite apart from the fact that we are likely to be most realistic if we begin with ourselves (most of us struggle in the same kind of areas), we cannot allow ourselves to forget that we are fellow disciples first and leaders only second.

- **Keep in line!**

Apply the passage consistently with the intended effect on the original readers. That is, ensure there is a 'straight line' that runs right through from the author's intentions (as far as we can discern them) to the effect you are looking for in the lives of yourself and your group members.

- **Keep the main thing the main thing!**

Make sure points of application derive from the central thrust of the passage. It is all too easy to be fascinated by asides, secondary points or assumptions in the text. Our diligent study will have been to no avail, though, if we go away shaping our lives from tangents in the text.

Articulate Your Goals

The second step in your preparation is to articulate very clearly the goals of understanding and application you want the group to leave with. This is, of course, simply a matter of summing up your earlier study of the passage. But it is worth being disciplined about this. It is no exaggeration to say this is probably the single most important step in your preparation. If you as a leader are not clear in your own mind what you want your members to be going away with, you can be sure they won't be impacted by God's word as profoundly as they might. Chances are they will come away with one of two inadequate reactions:

- 'Right but muddled'

  Those content to leave without tying up the loose ends will most likely leave 'right but muddled': they will have some vague idea about what the passage was saying and what they should do about it, but it is too hazy and ill-defined in their minds to make any definite response.

- 'Clear but wrong!'

  Those with tidier minds, whose natural tendency is always to straighten things out, will leave 'clear but wrong': they will be fairly confident about what the passage was saying and what they should do about it, but actually they have been allowed to draw incorrect conclusions, so their confidence is misplaced.

Given that this is such a crucial step to get right, it is worth crystallising these teaching goals in your mind so that they can be expressed in just a few concise sentences. Then write them down and have a good, long look at them! Try modifying and refining them, changing the wording slightly here and there until you are happy that they are a concise but precise summary of what the text says and what it implies for our beliefs, attitudes and behaviour.

Devise Your Observation Techniques

With teaching and application goals clearly articulated, the time has now come to turn your mind from the 'what' to the 'how'. Specifically, how are you going to lead the group in the direction of the goals you have identified? Given that everything comes from the passage itself, your first job must be to devise techniques to facilitate the group's observation of the passage. That is, you need to put your thinking cap on and work out how the group can be encouraged to rub their noses in it. The idea is for them to see for themselves what the text is (and is not) saying.

Here – more than anywhere else – is the place for as much freshness and imagination as you can possibly muster. There is, of course, no room for creativity in terms of the *content* of the study. Far from it. When you're coming up with *what* to communicate, the aim is to banish creativity as far as you can and allow the agenda to be set exclusively by the text. But now that you've moved on to thinking about *technique* and *how* to communicate that content, then it's fine to be as creative as you can!

There are just two general principles which need to guide you when you're thinking of ways to help group observation of the text.

The 'low-key' rule

Don't get so carried away with your observation method that too much attention ends up being focussed on the technique, leaving little left for the text itself! This can sometimes happen when particularly dramatic techniques (like interviews and role-play) are used. Procedures like these take a long time to set up and can easily either fall completely flat or end in uproar. Either way, the result is that, if not handled extremely well, all thoughts are drawn towards the drama of the thing. The text which they were supposed to illuminate ends up all but forgotten.

The 'variety' rule

Do make sure you use a good mixture of techniques so as to engage the attention of those whose minds work in different ways. We made the observation earlier that different people have different 'learning styles': some respond better to exercises involving seeing, hearing, or doing. When thinking about how to get people to connect with the text, the big temptation is to do it in either (i) the way you've seen it done in groups you've been part of in the past, or (ii) the way that works best for you personally. But if your group members are going to benefit most from the small group environment, you will need to ensure there is a good deal of diversity in your approach from week to week so that everybody finds things pitched at their wavelength regularly.

What, then, are some ways of rubbing noses in the text? The possibilities are endless, but among the more tried-and-tested, what follows are eight of the best.

1. Direct questions

One obvious technique is to use a mix of carefully-crafted questions to help people spot details in the text which they might easily have missed. Questions are, of course, the bread and butter of the small group leader. In fact, one of the things we may need to learn is to wean ourselves off spoken questions as our one-and-only method.

However, they do have an important place. They certainly place the largest burden on the leader's 'on the night' performance, and the success (or otherwise) of the observation exercise will depend very much on his or her sensitivity, skill, and general quick-wittedness. For all that, though, a well-phrased question can often be the fastest and most efficient means of getting the group to connect with the text in a fruitful way. We will think more about composing good questions when we come to interpretation a little later on. For the moment, however, just remember that our goal here is simply to try and work out what the text actually says, so we are aiming at simple comprehension questions.

Examples of good observation-questions

Genesis 1
'Look at what we're told about the activity of these first six days. What are some of the words and phrases which come up again and again each day?'

Ruth 1:1
'How does the writer date the story in the first verse?'

Luke 1:1-4
'Why does Luke set about writing his gospel, according to his opening paragraph?

Romans 1:1-4
'What key pieces of information do we find out in the opening verses about the message that Paul stands for?'

---

2. Clean text

For a longer study, you might find it helpful to provide group members with a 'clean' text (that is, one printed with no verse or chapter numbers and no section headings). With all the editorial 'helps' deleted, the group can work together to analyse the text's underlying theme, its flow and its key ideas. They might read it through a number of times – with pen or pencil in hand – either before or during the group time. The goal of the first read-through could be simply to spot recurring words and ideas in an attempt to come up with an initial impression of the underlying theme or themes. The second time, you could ask them to try and spot the key turning-points in order to identify the major subdivisions of the text (and perhaps provide titles to each). A third run-through will be a chance to have a closer look and see what information or data each of the subdivisions contributes to the major theme or themes.

Naturally, a good deal of discipline is needed from both the leader and the members to avoid getting bogged down in the nitty-gritty of particular words and phrases. (One way to do this is simply to appoint a scribe to write down such questions with a view to returning to them later.) But this kind of approach can be very helpful in getting to grips with a large block of text, for example, introducing the group to an entire book which is to be studied in greater detail over the weeks to come. If it is one of the shorter books (like Habakkuk or Titus), it might even be appropriate to use the marked sheets as the basis for all the ensuing studies. Note too that this style of study tends to appeal particularly to those of an artistic bent who feel they are 'making something' of the text; not so much to those who like everything properly ordered and presented.

Clean texts can be easily produced by any stand-ard computer Bible software or from a website like www.gospelcom.net. You may have to use word-processing software to help 'clean up', but this should be straightforward. Do watch out, though, for any copyright issues that may be involved by reproducing texts in this way.

3. Buzz-group summaries

Again, for relatively large passages, it may prove useful to split the members into pairs or threes in order to examine distinct portions of the text and attempt to summarise their findings for the wider group. Each reporting 'buzz-group' may then face questions from the others to probe and clarify their summaries.

This method has the great educational advantage of combining learning methods. Time is spent in individual reading, in discussing with one or two others, in distilling the material, in explaining (and defending) findings to others and then in listening to and engaging with the summaries provided by the different buzz-groups. It is particularly useful when used for *background* material to the main text under consideration. For example, it could well prove to be an efficient way to review the various episodes of the 'story so far' which are the backdrop to a particular event or climax. Or it might come in handy for summarising earlier events or passages which have a bearing on the study passage.

Buzz-groups tend to work best if you follow three guidelines:

- **Spell it out!**
  There's nothing worse than people not quite knowing what they're meant to be doing.

- Spot the leader!

As you divide up into groups, try to make sure there's one person in each who can take the initiative.

- Keep it snappy!

Better to finish without everything neatly tied up than to have some groups finish early and getting bored!

Examples of buzz-group summaries

Genesis 50:20
'Summarise the stories behind the phrases:
   (a) "you intended to harm me" (ch. 37-40) and
   (b) "the saving of many lives" (ch. 41-49).'

Hebrews 1
'What can you discover about the context of each of the OT quotes in this chapter?'

---

4. Summary tables

Some passages lend themselves to observation by means of tables which summarise simply and clearly the main points of content. The idea is to organise material into list form in order, for example, to help in making simple comparisons or contrasts, or just to get the key information into a form that's easy to interact with. Tables can be extremely helpful for the study: the work of filling them can be fun (especially for the more task-oriented members of the group) and provoke discussion (particularly when things in the passage aren't quite as neat as the table implies!). More than that, the completed table can provide a helpful visual basis from which to proceed in thrashing out application.

This technique can be used in almost any passage where some kind of extended contrast is made between two or more related ideas or characters. It can be done as a large group, in smaller buzz-groups or as individuals. As ever, a good, clear briefing is vital – the titles or questions you provide may seem as clear as day to you, but they may be as clear as mud to half the group!

Example of a summary table			
Luke 4:42-44 Look at the agenda-setting decision Jesus makes here. Fill in the table to get to the crux of it.			
	What he's deciding *against*	What he's deciding *for*	Key phrases and hints
1. What to prioritise			
2. Where to work			
3. Whom to please			
4. Which 'sphere' to favour			

5. *Everyday English Paraphrase*

It can often be helpful to 'unpack' the content of a verse – or even just one short phrase – by translating it into plainer, more everyday idiom. It might be that an expression can be so familiar that we unwittingly just gloss over it when we read it. So to regain the impact, we need to repackage the 'guts' of the word into an alternative expression with a little more punch. In other cases, the words on the page before us may be such jargon or so theologically technical that we need to translate it again just to make it comprehensible to our groups. Either way, this kind of 're-translating' is an invaluable technique and is likely to become a tool we will use very regularly.

There are two big traps that we'll need to be very careful not to fall into when we start paraphrasing the text in front of us:

- **Swapping jargon for gobbledegook?**
Beware coming up with something just as incomprehensible as what you started with. For example, it's all very well concluding that what Paul means by 'we have redemption through his blood' (Eph. 1:7) is that 'the self-satisfaction of God at the cross leads to a cessation of bondage to sin for his people'. That might clear things up very nicely for the person who made that contribution. But it probably won't get the rest of the group very far in their understanding.

- **Throwing out the baby with the bathwater?**
Beware of the beautiful, straightforward English paraphrase which is not actually a particularly helpful rendering of the text. For example to paraphrase 'In the beginning was the Word' (John 1:1) as 'Jesus was around from the start of time' is really a step backwards, not forwards. It misses the whole point of why John uses that 'Word' language.

> ## Examples of everyday English paraphrase
>
> Mark 8:29
> 'What is Peter really saying when he declares, "You are the Christ"?'
>
> Colossians 1:15
> 'Can you unpack that expression Paul uses: "The firstborn over all creation"?'

6. Pictures and Diagrams

There are no pictures in the Bible. If your edition has them in, they come as an added extra, courtesy of the publishers! That said, there are many occasions when the Bible writers seem to expect us to visualise what they describe. It might be simple use of 'word-pictures', detailed descriptions, specific instructions or graphic imagery of some other kind. Often the picture is quite 'impressionist': perhaps we're simply meant to be bowled over by the grandeur of the scene that's described. In other cases, though, it can be helpful to try and convert the description into some kind of picture or diagram. That is, it's a means of rubbing our noses in the text and helping us to work out what it says.

Because this is one of the more adventurous observation techniques, it's worth bearing in mind a couple of simple guidelines to make sure the exercise isn't a complete flop.

- Get the kit!

  Make sure you have everything the group will need for the exercise. Appropriate pens and paper are vital. A photocopied outline may be useful to give people a good start.

- Spare the klutz!

Do be sensitive to artistic incompetence. Try and defuse the inevitable 'I can't draw' objections by stressing that the benefit is the exercise itself, not the quality of the end product. If you think that even then some may be just plain embarrassed, then give this technique a skip!

Examples of drawings and pictures

1 Kings 6
'Have a go at drawing a diagram of the temple, or at least its floor plan. Use Hebrews 9:1-5 as a guide to the most important features.'

Acts 13-28
Distribute a map of the Mediterranean with key places marked on it. 'Chart Paul's journey on each of his three missionary journeys.'

---

7. Diagramming sentences

Most of the Bible translations in large-scale use today do us a favour when it comes to long and complicated sentences. They tend to break them down into rather more manageable units. Sometimes, though, if we're completely honest, it feels as though they could have done a better job. We know what Peter means when he says Paul's letters 'contain some things that are hard to understand'!(2 Pet. 3:16)

One very useful technique to help us get to the heart of such difficult sentences is sentence-diagramming. The idea is to spread the sentence over a number of lines, using indentation and arrows to work out the sense. When it's laid out like this, it's easy to spot what the key issues being addressed are, and what information is given about those issues.

There are a few basic rules:

- Start writing the sentence at the top left corner of a page.

- Every time you come to a new thing that's said (maybe a new sentence or a 'but' or an 'and' etc.), which has no particular relationship with what's been said immediately before, start a new line.

- Every time you come to a sub-idea that gives further information about a main idea that's already been mentioned, start a new line but

  (a) indent the sub-idea
  (b) put an arrow between the sub-idea and the main idea
  (c) underline the main idea which has been expanded. (You may need lots of indentations!)

- Whenever you come to the end of an indented sub-idea, continue on going back to the previous appropriate indent.

- You may have to 'cheat' occasionally in the layout just to fit it all on the page!

It sounds complicated, but actually you'll get the hang of it pretty quickly. Once you've done one, it's easy. Have a look at Titus 2:11-14 as an example.

> [11]For the grace of God that brings salvation has appeared to all men. [12]It teaches us to say "No" to ungodliness and worldly passions, and to live self-controlled, upright and godly lives in this present age, [13]while we wait for the

blessed hope--the glorious appearing of our great God and Saviour, Jesus Christ, [14]who gave himself for us to redeem us from all wickedness and to purify for himself a people that are his very own, eager to do what is good.

At first sight, it might look impenetrable. But look at it in diagram form.

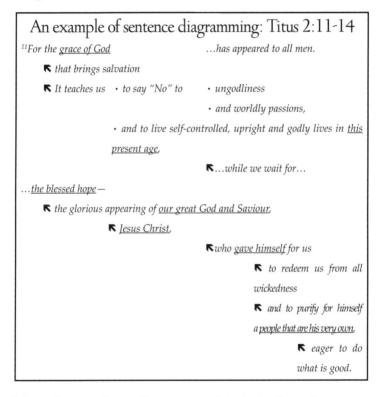

An example of sentence diagramming: Titus 2:11-14

[11]*For the <u>grace of God</u>*   *...has appeared to all men.*

     ↖ *that brings salvation*

     ↖ *It teaches us*   • *to say "No" to*   • *ungodliness*

                                      • *and worldly passions,*

                    • *and to live self-controlled, upright and godly lives in <u>this present age</u>,*

                             ↖*...while we wait for...*

...<u>the blessed hope</u>—

    ↖ *the glorious appearing of <u>our great God and Saviour</u>,*

         ↖ <u>*Jesus Christ,*</u>

                 ↖*who <u>gave himself</u> for us*

                      ↖ *to redeem us from all wickedness*

                      ↖ *and to purify for himself <u>a people that are his very own</u>,*

                         ↖ *eager to do what is good.*

Now that we have diagrammed it, it is clear that most of the 'information' is related to two key issues: *God's grace* and *our hope*. We can now devote some time in our study to working through exactly what is said about these subjects.

8. Logical Flow Diagrams

This is a similar approach to sentence diagramming, but it follows the logic of the *ideas* instead of the detail of the *grammar*. The principle is once again to repackage the flowing prose of the text in front of us into a simple visual format in order to aid basic comprehension of the text and, in particular, to help understand the connection between blocks of material.

Depending on the group – and the passage – it may sometimes be helpful to provide members with outline flow-diagrams, i.e. a photocopy of the boxes, arrows and connecting words which form the skeleton of the diagram you are hoping to end up with. In other cases, you may like to start with a completely blank sheet and work together to construct the diagram.

Again, you may often like to work with the text itself. Alternatively, perhaps where it is particularly unwieldy, you may like to work with summaries of the ideas contained in it.

Once again, an example may help. Romans 1:16-20 is an example of a tightly argued passage of Paul.

> [16]I am not ashamed of the gospel, because it is the power of God for the salvation of everyone who believes: first for the Jew, then for the Gentile. [17]For in the gospel a righteousness from God is revealed, a righteousness that is by faith from first to last, just as it is written: "The righteous will live by faith." [18] [For] The wrath of God is being revealed from heaven against all the godlessness and wickedness of men who suppress the truth by their wickedness, [19]since what may be known about God is plain to them, because God has made it plain to them. [20]For since the creation of the world God's invisible qualities--his eternal power and divine nature--have been clearly seen, being understood from what has been made, so that men are without excuse.

Helpfully, most of the logical links are spelt out in the NIV
– the only one that is omitted is the 'For' at the beginning of
verse 18. But again it's pretty dense stuff without separating
it out.

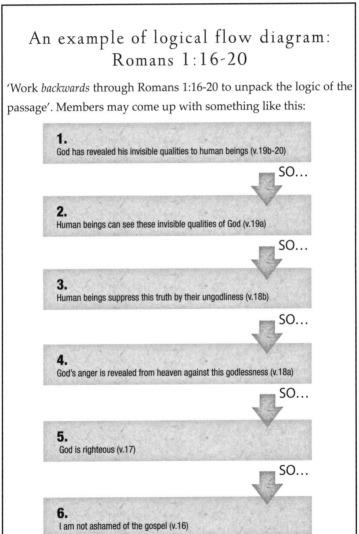

An example of logical flow diagram: Romans 1:16-20

'Work *backwards* through Romans 1:16-20 to unpack the logic of the passage'. Members may come up with something like this:

1.
God has revealed his invisible qualities to human beings (v.19b-20)

SO...

2.
Human beings can see these invisible qualities of God (v.19a)

SO...

3.
Human beings suppress this truth by their ungodliness (v.18b)

SO...

4.
God's anger is revealed from heaven against this godlessness (v.18a)

SO...

5.
God is righteous (v.17)

SO...

6.
I am not ashamed of the gospel (v.16)

Craft Your Interpretation Questions

So far, we have simply looked at ways to introduce the group to what the text *says*. In other words, when you put these techniques to work, they should lead to an understanding of the words, phrases, characters and ideas brought up by the text as well as the logical connection between those ideas. By this stage, they should be pretty well acquainted with the text.

The next stage is to lead the group towards an understanding of what it all *means*. That is, the time has come to translate their discoveries into concepts. We are beginning to move from the particulars of the text to the universals of the Bible's message. The broad question we are posing now is: what, in the context of the book and of the Bible as a whole, does the text mean? So, whatever weird and wonderful techniques we may have employed to survey the text, now is the time for just one thing: talk!

1. The importance of good interpretation questions

Remember why we are doing Bible study in a small group context in the first place. It's not primarily because the small group is a nice, manageable social unit or because it's just the right size to get into our living rooms. We adopt the small-group format in simple recognition of a basic fact: people tend to learn something more thoroughly when they discover it and articulate it themselves than when they hear somebody else explain it.

That means the questions we ask are absolutely vital. If people are learning lessons by thinking and speaking, it's crucial that what we ask them to think and speak *about* are the right issues and that we give them enough guidance to speak correctly about those issues.

As a skilful leader, you will try to tread a fine line between two common errors of approach when it comes to just how much guidance to give.

- ### The 'free-for-all' approach
Leaving the group to feel their own way blindly along is not going to be very productive. They might have great fun along the way but, as often as not, they'd never actually make it to their destination! The 'free-for-all' approach might lead to a lively group discussion, but the members are likely to leave none the wiser about what God is actually saying in the text they have been studying.

- ### The 'schoolteacher' approach
On the other hand, you won't want to dictate every single move to them at every point along the way. The group might reach the destination alright, but they may as well have been led along by the hand with a blindfold over their heads. In other words, the heavy-handed 'schoolteacher' approach may leave them quite clear about the main points of the passage, but they may as well have listened to a sermon rather than sat down to an interactive group discussion.

As one who has spent some time traipsing around the woods to find the way through (and locating the potholes and blind alleys), you will give your group enough freedom to feel they are making real discoveries for themselves, but enough direction to bring them to where your own pioneering intensive study has shown you they ought to be heading.

2. Principles for interpretation questions

As you become more experienced as a small group leader, you'll instinctively shape your studies in a way that is helpful to others. That includes the questions you ask. You'll learn what kinds of question lead to the most fruitful discussions. However, here a few guidelines to get you going!

- ### Keep the ball in play

  Some questions are open; others are closed. Open questions are those which open up discussion. That is, they lead to thoughtful reflection, open debate, and different opinions, so they engage the attention of the group and keep people talking. Closed questions are those which close down discussion. They have a single right answer (which is often embarrassingly obvious) and they're often about as interesting and engaging as watching paint dry.

Examples of closed questions

Mark 4:1-20
'How many types of soil are there?'

Romans 4
'Was Abraham justified by faith or works?'

Examples of open questions

Mark 4:1-20
'How does Jesus describe the different types of soil?'

Romans 4
'What possibilities does Paul discuss for how Abraham might have been justified?'

Closed questions do have their place. In particular, they may be needed more for those not used to basic comprehension of texts or free discussion. Sometimes too it will be necessary to backtrack from a difficult open question to a series of simple closed questions in order to help the group to answer the original open question. But on the whole, they are best kept to a minimum.

• **Keep your passes short**

If you're going to keep the discussion of the text moving forward, the last thing you want is for people to get stuck on the complexity of your questions.

Sometimes the problem will be length. We mistakenly think that we can get a good discussion going by asking three questions in one. Such 'long balls', however, generally confuse and end up focussing attention on the question rather than the text. Take it one step at a time.

At other times the problem is our wording. We unwittingly use pieces of theological jargon or obscure vocabulary. At best, people will ask what we mean and we will have to rephrase. At worst, half the group will just be embarrassed and stay quiet, leaving only the know-alls to interact with you.

Examples of over-complicated questions

Luke 1:67-79
'Look at what we learn here about Jesus' redemption. When was it promised, by whom, from what, for what and who is it announced by?'

Psalm 139
'What life-circumstances precipitate a need for certainty about divine transcendence?'

- **Keep your nose down**

One of the dangers of the small-group format comes from its superficial similarity to other kinds of group that members may have been part of in the past. Such groups abound: there are self-help groups, focus groups, therapy groups, reading groups and so on. The emphasis of such groups is generally on *my* feelings, *my* reactions and *my* opinions. It is important to be aware that this kind of ethos may be part of the baggage people are bringing into our small groups.

So we need to work hard at keeping people's noses in the text. That means trying to phrase questions, on the whole, in such a way that they cannot be answered from pure general knowledge or personal opinion. If you do need to draw on people's wider knowledge of the Bible or the world at large, it's good to bounce off from something in the passage. Similarly, if you are specifically looking for personal opinions at any particular point, it is best to try and hook it into the text.

If people still fail to engage with the text, despite your prompts, they might need to be brought back to it with follow-up questions like 'Where is that in the text?' or (perhaps less aggressively) 'Was there a particular verse you had in mind?' The text is our guide. We are not looking for people to play their own game, with their own subjective rules, but to anchor everything in the text we've been given.

Examples of nose-up questions

Genesis 3:1-7
'Why do you think Eve ate the fruit?'

Philippians 2:1-11
'What does Christian unity mean?'

Examples of nose-down questions

Genesis 3:1-7
'What were the stages leading up to Eve eating the fruit?'

Philippians 2:1-11
'How does Paul break down what Christian unity involves?'

• **Keep your eyes on the goal**

As you work through the text, there are bound to be important issues emerging which are not necessarily the main point of the passage. That is, they are more important to group members than to the Bible writer's purpose. Clearly these need to be addressed – if only by acknowledging them and promising a discussion over coffee! In fact, if they are not so addressed, they are likely to prove distracting. Similarly we'll need to think about the tricky verses ahead of time, so that we can help those who are perplexed by them.

For the most part, however, in formulating questions, we need to be goal-driven. We discussed at the beginning of this chapter the importance of articulating clear goals for the study. We now need to make sure that the burden of our questions is actually related to that goal. In other words our job is not to squeeze out every last bit of theological juice from each verse but to lead people to the heart of the passage.

As an example, consider a climactic moment in Mark's gospel.

[27]Jesus and his disciples went on to the villages around Caesarea Philippi. On the way he asked them, "Who do people say I am?" [28]They replied, "Some say John the Baptist; others say Elijah; and still others, one of the prophets." [29]"But what about you?" he asked. "Who do you say I am?" Peter answered, "You are the Christ." [30]Jesus warned them not to tell anyone about him.

(Mark 8:27-30)

Example of a 'random' question

'Who does Mark mean by Jesus' "disciples"? Can you remember some of their names?'

Example of a goal-driven question

'Think back over the gospel so far. What do you think it was about Jesus that led Peter to come to this conclusion?'

---

3. Different types of interpretation questions

With these general principles in place, it is time to consider some of the different kinds of questions that might make up your armoury. We have already discussed 'observation' questions. The kind of quest-ions we're considering here generally assume such observation work. It is not an exhaustive list: some profitable questions you might ask don't really fit into any of these categories, or else overlap two or more of them. However, it is worth noting that a good study is likely to include a mix of what follows.

- Kick-off questions

Here is a sobering truth. A tired group member will often unconsciously decide whether or not to make the effort to engage with the entire study according to whether the very first question commands his or her attention. So it is crucial to get it right. A good kick-off question will generally be …

(a) *Attention-grabbing.* Although the Bible is *always* relevant, we often need to be reminded of its relevance!

(b) *Goal-related.* It's helpful, right from the beginning, to give people a 'hook' on which to hang what they learn.

(c) *Open-ended.* The idea is to get people into the mode of talking and discussing spiritually-important things.

Example of a poor kick-off question

Mark 8:27-30
'Can anybody remember what last week's study was about?'

Example of a good kick-off question

Mark 8:27-30
'If you did a survey of your work-colleagues over your lunch break and asked them what they thought of Jesus, what sort of things do you think they'd say?'

- Probing questions

These are questions that get to the nub of the issue behind the text. In other words, they encourage members to dig deeper under the surface to discover the fundamental point that's being made by the Bible writer. They assume the 'concrete' and move to the 'abstract'.

Examples of probing questions

Isaiah 40:18
'What's the writer trying to say when he asks: "To whom will you compare God?" '

Hebrews 1:5-14
'What point is the writer trying to get across by this mass of Old Testament quotations?'

• **Context questions**

We thought earlier about how the point of a passage is often only discovered when it is set in its context. These kinds of questions try to get group members to do exactly that. They link the text to what surrounds it (either immediately or in the whole book or even the whole Bible) to tease out what the text must therefore mean.

If these kinds of questions are not asked, the consequences can be disastrous for understanding the passage. For example, when Jesus says, 'As the Father has sent me, I am sending you' (John 20:21), does that mean Christian believers are to do exactly the same things as Jesus (healings, exorcisms, dying on a cross)? People might think so, unless a couple of context questions are asked: 'What is the language of "sending" all about in John's gospel so far?' (answer:

obedience) and 'Who is the "you" that Jesus is talking about?' (answer: the Twelve).

In some cases, it might actually be the doctrinal framework of the whole Bible we need to appeal to as relevant context. For example, when James writes, 'a person is justified by what he does and not by faith alone' (James 2:24), does that really mean we can get right with God by performance alone? Surely not! We will need to clear that up, by saying for example, 'Flick back to Ephesians 2:1-10. How does what Paul says here qualify James 2:24?'

Examples of context questions

Ruth 1:22
'Why do you think the writer refers to the start of the "barley harvest"? Look back at verse 1.'

Philippians 2:6
'What do those words, "did not consider equality with God something to be grasped" say about the question of whether Jesus was or was not God? How does the rest of the New Testament help us here?'

Titus 3:9
'What do you suppose these "foolish controversies" might be about? How does 1:10-16 help us pin them down?'

• **Summary questions**

These are questions which round up all the observations made so far and try to distil them into central principles. This is the stage at which we lead the group very deliberately to a grasp of our main teaching goals. However much our group members enjoy the study, it will only actually be profitable to them if they can remember the thrust of the passage. If we do not spend time summarising, they are likely to remember either nothing or only incidentals.

We will most likely need to attempt 'mini-summaries' two or three times during the course of a study, as well as a 'maxi-summary' at the end. Mini-summaries attempt to refocus attention on a main idea after spending time exploring sub-themes or having an extended discussion. Maxi-summaries wrap up everything that has been learnt during the course of the study.

Examples of summary questions

Luke 3:21-4:13
'Just to recap, then, what's the common thread we've seen again and again through Jesus' baptism, genealogy and temptation?'

2 Peter 2
'So in all that detail, what are the key points Peter wants to make about false teachers?'

Consider Areas of Application

The time has now come to encourage the group to respond in their lives to the truths which have been discovered. As ever, the response we are looking for is not a subjective one, but is one in line with what the text itself demands. Indeed, we might more helpfully talk of 'implications' of the text rather than 'applications', since the former expression seems to express the close connection between text and response better.

In some cases, it might not be appropriate to move to this 'endgame' until the end of the study. For example, often with Old Testament narrative, it can be dangerous to move to application before considering the entire story. Generally, though, we will want to anchor the text in our lives by stepping back to apply it repeatedly on the way through. Remember the three basic types of application: truths to be believed (*mind-application*), attitudes to be fostered (*heart-application*) and behaviour to be modified (*will-application*). Let us consider how we can move towards each in turn.

1. Truths to be believed

The first, and perhaps most basic, response we are looking for to any text is a change of mind. Everybody has a worldview. They come to the study with a great number of assumptions and beliefs about God, the world and human beings. If the passage has been shown to contradict that world-view, then our members have a simple choice: to confirm their original worldview (and thereby rebel against God) or to change their worldview (and thereby submit to God). Naturally we greatly desire as leaders that they do the latter. But we need to show them how. So we need to use simple questions to tease out very clearly what truths are to be believed and, in particular, where these truths conflict with the opinions people currently hold.

A secondary aim of these mind-application questions is to help members to organise and articulate their beliefs. That is, if we asked them in the right language, we might discover they do already hold to this or that biblical truth. But their thinking has never been clear on the subject, and they certainly wouldn't be able to explain lucidly their position to anybody else. These questions, then, serve to confirm and clarify their beliefs and to enable them to communicate them to others.

There is generally no room for subtlety in any application questions, and certainly not in these mind-applications. So it's helpful to ask straightforward questions: 'So what does this passage say to somebody who thinks X?' or 'How is verse 10 a rebuke to those of us who tend to think of God as Y?'

Examples of mind-application questions

John 16:5-16
'Many people think the New Testament is just a bunch of human documents reflecting human opinions. How do these verses challenge that belief?'

Romans 3:9-20
'What do these verses say to those of us who like to think of human beings as fundamentally good?'

---

2. Attitudes to be fostered

Some of those who are strong on the Bible have a tendency to be *light on feeling*. We might agree that God's saving actions are wonderful, but we hold back from getting really excited about them. Or we could feel some shame at our innate sinfulness, but we rarely find ourselves utterly horrified by it. Perhaps we articulate our gratitude to God for his fatherly provision for us, but we don't wake up every morning longing to say 'thank you' to God in some new way.

Of course many hide behind culture to explain away this reserve. But if it is culture that is restraining us from responding to God appropriately, we may need to learn to identify more with Christ than with our culture. Culture is not neutral. It never has been. It is nothing but an expression of human attitudes and therefore is infected with sin from beginning to end.

So we cannot rely on our members responding appropriately to what they learn by gut instinct. They need to be encouraged to be deliberate in fostering fitting heart-responses to the lessons learnt in the Bible study. Because we are all natural Pharisees and prefer to concentrate on measurable, quantifiable applications, some may find it hard to talk honestly about this kind of response. This does not make it optional, though. Rather, it just means we may need to work hard at helping them to do so.

Examples of heart-application questions

John 16:5-16
'How ought we to respond to a God who goes to such lengths to ensure we have reliable information about him and his plans?'

Romans 3:9-20
'In the light of these verses, what kind of attitude should we have towards ourselves and our behaviour and motivations?'

---

3. Behaviour to be modified

This is where the crunch really comes. Whether or not we are really prepared to change the way we live is a good test of whether we are really putting our money where our mouth is in our Christian commitment. So although in one sense our behaviour is no more important than our beliefs and attitudes, we do need to prepare well to ensure the lesson hits home on the ground-level of how we spend our time, money, energy, leisure, words and so on.

Don't forget a simple ABC of will-application:

- Be *alert*

Some lifestyle issues are pretty sensitive for some – notably sexual misbehaviour, but also attitudes towards alcohol and money. There is a danger that defensive people in this situation may feel they are being picked on. You just need to know the group and be wise. (This is where one-to-one pastoral contact becomes invaluable.)

- Be *bold*

The subject matter might be rather delicate, but we do not have license to duck the hard ones (or even just 'fail to leave time for application'!) And don't be afraid to revisit issues. If the book we're studying week after week addresses the same topics again and again, it does so for a reason.

- Be *concrete*

Most of us are reasonably aware of our failures and the best way to hide them is to talk in generalities rather than specifics. The Bible study is not necessarily the best time to encourage people to own up to their shameful behaviour in all areas of life, but the leader will need to take the lead in personal honesty in particular areas.

Examples of will-application questions

Philippians 1:12-26
'What practical steps can we take to develop an evangelistic lifestyle like Paul's?'

Luke 12:13-21
'What is there about the way we spend our money that reflects the materialism of the rich fool?'

5

Leading the Meeting

There is nothing quite like stage-fright. A recent survey found that public speaking is the number one fear among adults. It topped fear of flying, fear of sickness, fear of financial problems and even fear of death! It was found to affect not only the timid and socially anxious, but also those who present as confident and outgoing, even accomplished entertainers. People go to huge lengths to avoid up-front speaking.

Leading a small group Bible study is not quite the same as giving a speech before a throng of hundreds. Nevertheless it can strike fear into the most surprising people. Many of us would much rather spend hours working with the text on our own than be faced with a room full of people looking to us for leadership and teaching. However, with some thought and careful preparation the task is not as daunting as we might have feared! In particular, we need to think through six aspects of what happens 'on the night'.

Setting the Scene

The place is tidy. The kettle is on. We are looking presentable. The doorbell's going to ring any moment with the first arrivals. We are feeling on top of things, with only a tinge of panic. Now is the time to think: what have I forgotten? Time to run down this checklist.

1. Remember the practicalities

All sorts of factors can throw a study off course or make for a generally poor outcome. Some of these are just plain unforeseeable. Others, however, can be prevented with just a little forethought.

One of the key things to get right is the *seating arrangement*. This might seem surprisingly trivial, but it can affect the study dramatically. The golden rule is: eye-contact encourages people to speak; no eye-contact discourages it. So we need to try, without being too forced and artificial about it, to place the noisier types next to us and the more timid (as well as the co-leader) opposite us.

Attention paid to the *atmosphere* of the room will similarly reap dividends. Rather than wait until it's stifling or freezing, think ahead and do what it takes to get the temperature right before you start. If in doubt, it's best to err on the cool side. Certainly, a good movement of air is helpful to aid concentration. And while you are at it, think about lighting. The print in Bibles is often painfully small, so to help people read easily, make sure there's no lack of wattage on the bulb front. The subtle side-lights approach might do the trick for that plush dinner party. But for a Bible study, bring on the floodlights!

2. Remember who's the boss

Now that the atmospherics are sorted out and people are seated in the right spot, it's time to begin the meeting. How do we do that? If we think of our small group as primarily a forum for information to be exchanged, we'll most likely get our Bibles out, read the passage and get to work. However, if we remember that it is God who inspired the text and he alone who can make it clear to us, then the only appropriate place to begin is with *prayer*. We will ask God to give us concentration, clarity of thought, understanding and the humility to be shaped by what we learn.

Incidentally, we are likely to continue to come up against this tendency to see Bible study primarily in terms of education and learning. One helpful way to combat it is to be as consistent as possible in the vocabulary to describe what we're doing. For example, try avoiding expressions like 'studying the Bible' and plump instead for 'listening to God'.

3. Remember your role
One of the most widespread errors to be made in Bible-study groups is for the leader to think the group does not actually need clear leadership. Sometimes this is just an excuse for those who naturally find it hard to take charge. Other times it results from the mistaken conviction that 'the Spirit will lead' without using any human agent. Either way, the result is often disastrous. At best, an aimless free-for-all discussion takes place, dominated by the more talkative individuals, which leaves everyone disappointed and frustrated. At worst, the passage is allowed to be misread, the group is therefore seriously misled, and serious doctrinal error goes unchecked.

The remedy for all this is for the leader to display strong leadership. We leaders are not merely discussion-facilitators or chairpersons of a committee. We are goal-driven leaders, who need to steer the discussion subtly but deliberately towards an understanding of what God is communicating through the passage, and to the response that he demands. Be prepared, then, to play that role. Interrupt fruitless discussion, steer people back to the point, challenge and question contributions and generally take a lead. It may feel unnatural, especially when members are very much our peers, but the group will thank us in the end!

Teasing out the Truth

On the whole, we will find that when we throw open questions into the ring, the first answer will not be 'the truth, the whole truth and nothing but the truth'. Often far from it! A good deal of further exploration, then, will be needed. This means we need to think carefully about our strategy for pushing the discussion on towards the destination we're aiming at. In particular, three principles should govern our approach.

1. Think on your feet

First of all, we need to be able to be quick-witted. We need to think on our feet so as to be able to make quick decisions about how to advance things. Now, of course, for some of us, this is our great forte; for others, it certainly doesn't come naturally. There are, however, a few things we can do to help.

- Get a good night's sleep.
  That is the first rule. There is no point poring over the text until the early hours if it's going to leave us zombie-like in the meeting next day.

- Remember the final destination.
  If we have drilled ourselves in what our main teaching goal is, as well as what the 'scaffolding

points' are, it will make instinctive questioning much easier.

- **Use a crib sheet.**

We can go into the study with the finest, most skilful questions imaginable, but it won't get us far if we can't remember the answers we had in mind. Try jotting down in note form the key points you're trying to get at by your questions.

Do avoid overkill, though. If somebody gives all the information we're looking for – though not quite in the same terms we might have used – we need not 'cap' their answers. Let them stand. Affirm what they have discovered or realised for themselves in the words they use.

2. *Keep asking questions*

It may be that the discussion is just not going in the direction we planned, or even anywhere close! This can be pretty disconcerting, particularly if we are less confident and experienced. The temptation at this point is simply to come in and answer your own question: 'What I was driving at was ...' Alternatively, as the discussion proceeds, someone may ask you a question from the passage directly. Again, the temptation is to offer an answer.

Don't do it! For a good discussion to take place, some adrenalin and unresolved tension is required. But if the leader answers the question, both are reduced and, as a consequence, the discussion quickly comes to a shuddering halt. Our job is to help the group members come up with the answers themselves, simply by asking them the right questions.

Two simple rules are:

- Cross the ball, don't score the goal.

In other words, set somebody else up to give the right answer. For example, point them to a particular verse or remind them of something that's been said which might help them.

- Answer questions with questions.

That is, try your hardest not to give straight answers. Instead, either throw the question out to the group as a whole ('Who can help Jimmy with that one?') or again supply the asker with a piece of the jigsaw rather than the finished product ('Does verse 18 help us there?')

Coping with Contributions

Let's backtrack just a little. Somebody has said something – anything – in response to a question we've asked. It may have been sensible; it may have been off the wall. What are the things to bear in mind in general when we're responding?

1. Any contribution

Whatever anybody says, the first thing is to acknowledge the contribution. But it's not quite as simple as that. We need to do it in such a way that the contributor *feels* acknowledged. That is, although we might think a simple 'Hmmm' or grunt is enough, that kind of reaction may not convince the contributor that you've really engaged with what they've said. If they're not so convinced, the result may be that they feel unvalued and so become less inclined to speak again.

You shouldn't go too far wrong, though, if you follow a couple of simple rules.

- *Catch their eyes.* Sustained eye-contact is as affirming, if not more so, than a great gush of words!

- *Use their words.* Reflect some of their own phraseology back to them, and they're unlikely to think you haven't listened.

2. Poor contributions

Coping with answers that are just plain wrong is one of the toughest challenges facing the small group leader. It is particularly difficult with individuals who find it hard to distinguish between a rejection of their opinion and a rejection of them as a person. So we must tread carefully.

As a basic rule of thumb, never flatly contradict any contribution, however hopeless it might be. To say a member is wrong in front of the group may be so crushing that the contributor never opens his or her mouth again for the rest of the study! Instead, try and work with what they've said as the basis for further exploration. This is easier said than done and is, in fact, something of an art form. It may, though, be worth trying one of the following:

- **Spot something good**
  Latch on to a part of their answer but challenge the rest, e.g. 'Yes, I think you're right in that it's to do with "Jesus", but is it actually his "sinlessness" or something else about him?'

- **Throw it open**

Ask for other people's opinions: 'What do others think?'

- **Full-scale retreat.**

Be non-committal and retreat to a series of simple, closed questions in order to build up to the question more slowly, e.g. 'That's certainly one possibility. Have another look at verse 6. What's the first thing Jesus says to them?'

3. Good contributions

Once again, there's a temptation here that we need to try not to give in to. When somebody gives a good answer, don't say so too quickly. If our approval is too quick and too decisive, that will close down discussion and the focus will shift to the leader once again. The effect of this is a very stop-start, leader-focussed dynamic, which can be unhelpful. If we try instead to be slightly more tentative in our endorsement of the contribution, that leaves the door open for further reflection among the group as a whole.

4. No contribution

It will happen. So we may as well be prepared for it. We ask our carefully-worded, text-engaging, searching question and … nothing but a dreadful silence! The less experienced we are, the more terrified we tend to be of long pauses. A couple of points are worth bearing in mind.

- **It's not actually that long**

On the whole, we're not good at judging time in these circumstances. The silence is generally not nearly as long as we think it is. If in doubt, cast a furtive glance at your watch after asking a question. That ten minute silence that we feel is likely to be only ten seconds in fact.

- **It's not actually that bad**

Silence probably means that you've simply asked a question that demands thought. And thought is a good thing! So resist the temptation to jump in with another question too quickly. Rather, defuse the atmosphere by acknowledging the complexity of the issue: 'That's a hard one, isn't it? Let me give you a little longer to think about it.'

- **When all else fails, rephrase**

If the silence really is getting embarrassing to the extent that people (not just you) are looking uncomfortable, just give a little bit of help by rephrasing the question slightly – it might make all the difference!

Handling the Hijackers

'My small group would be just fine if it weren't for the people in the group.' Few would be as bold as to say something like that, but many of us have felt it at times. The problem is, all that hard work and planning we put into our studies seems to be in vain as, again and again, people just don't say the things they're meant to!

There are a few common roles that people play in any group that can have a detrimental effect on the discussion. It's worth having a strategy for how to cope with each of them.

1. Simon the Spectator

There are always going to be some who are quieter than others in any given group. This is usually an expression of personality rather than spirituality. Some are simply less confident than others. However, if for a sustained period a member has made virtually no verbal contribution to the discussion, it is likely that he or she is not getting the most out of the group. More than that, their silent presence may cause uneasiness among other members. The time has come to take action!

Eye contact is an obvious first port of call. Make sure you sit down opposite them in the group and try to look at them frequently when asking questions. Watch out for occasions when they are trying to enter the discussion but are finding it difficult to get their bit in. If that doesn't do the trick, try the 'ramp-up' approach. Ease them in gently to speaking in the group context by asking them to read the passage, then by addressing them directly with simple, straightforward questions. Then there is the 'write down and read' trick. From time to time, invite the group to think through their answer to a question and write it down so that all take it in turns to read their answer. Whatever you do, be appreciative and encouraging when they do say something. If they still sit in stony silence, you may need to have a quiet word with them to see if there is a particular issue they are struggling with (e.g. boredom or feeling intimidated) and address the situation accordingly.

2. Charlie the Chatterbox

For every one spectator, there's always at least one chatterbox. Whether they're driven by insecurity or ego-mania or simply a love for the sound of their own voice, they just don't seem capable of shutting up, so that nobody else can get a word in edgeways!

You will need to be gentle but firm with the chatterbox. Try *asking others to speak* on occasion: 'somebody who hasn't spoken yet', or – if necessary – 'anybody else apart from Charlie'. As a last resort, you may have to *interrupt the monologue*: when he or she pauses for breath, take the opportunity to thank them and move on to something else. If they remain unresponsive to your hints, look for an opportunity to point out privately the effect of their garrulousness on the group and encourage them to serve the group better by holding back.

3. Danielle the Digresser

There are those who can focus on the text in front of them and then there are those who – well – just can't! Some people seem to be able to spot a tangent a mile off and cannot stop themselves from hijacking the discussion. Such red herrings can be very interesting topics of conversation, and indeed can serve to bring some of the spectators out of their shells. But they can too easily dominate the whole meeting, so need to be dealt with firmly.

The main, tried-and-tested line of attack on digressions is *postponement*. Encourage the digresser to bring up the topic over coffee or at the group's next social meeting. Sometimes all that is necessary is to *refocus*. Simply pointing out that the discussion has gone slightly off-track may be all that's needed to bring people back to the text.

4. Eddie the Expert

Some people just have all the answers perfectly worked out. They know it all. In fact you find yourself wondering why they even bother to turn up to your home group! Of course it can be great to have somebody like that in the group. But it can also be pretty intimidating for others.

There are two main options for dealing with the expert. One is to *use them*. Give them a role as a deputy leader. Perhaps invite them to prepare and give a short presentation on a subject that has come up in discussion. Or focus on training them to lead a group of their own. The other option is to *gag them*. If they are expansive in sharing their wisdom, then you may need to deal with them as a 'Charlie the Chatterbox' (see above).

5. *Harry the Humorist*

Ah, yes. Finally, there is the comedian. Maybe you have one of these in your group: one who suffers from 'terminal humour'. There's a witty riposte ready and waiting for any occasion; he or she can cause a ripple of laughter with no effort at all. Actually it's often great to have one of these types around. It stops the group growing too intense. It relieves tension and makes everyone more relaxed. And it can have a great 'feel-good' effect on the group in general.

If the humorist is attracting too much attention, however, then he or she may need calming down a little. Try *the straight face approach*. Deliberately make a point of not laughing at the gag and carry on the discussion ignoring the joke. Or it may be that the *deep probe* is necessary. There may be a spiritual issue which underlies the humour to do with insecurity or a need to deflect attention from serious engagement.

Directing the Dynamics

If members are going to contribute freely and give something of themselves, they need to feel at ease. Nobody's going to give 100 per cent if they're worried about how others will react to what they're saying. The whole dynamic just won't be right. There are certain ground rules that need to be laid out from study number one (and repeated often). In particular there are three ingredients that make for a secure environment, and we as leaders need to take responsibility for them all.

1. An atmosphere of trust.

Sensitive issues are bound to come up in the course of discussion. We need, therefore, to insist on absolute confidentiality among all members about issues which are explicitly flagged up as confidential. But more than that, members need to develop an instinct for issues that are best not broadcast. The wounds of a single confidence betrayed can take a long time to heal.

But just as important as guarding tongues outside the group environment, members need to learn to watch what they say inside. If somebody is sensitive on an issue, it can take great courage to speak about it openly. The journey to that moment will be shortened, though, if he or she can observe a pattern of supportive and non-condemning reactions to the contributions of others. Each must be committed to valuing and affirming one another, being quick to listen and slow to judge. We leaders will need to set the pace here; if we do, others will generally pick up from us.

2. An atmosphere of harmony

As we've seen in an earlier chapter, it's helpful to agree as a group on what the group's goals are going to be, so as not to allow frustration to develop. But there are also relationship issues. There are often one or two who just can't seem to help being wound up by one another. As the weeks go by, the group leader will need to be on the look-out for such harmful personality clashes and take appropriate action (i.e. have a quiet word!).

3. An atmosphere of loyalty

The members need to agree on the priority they will give to attendance of the group and to the relationships they have with one another. There are few things more discouraging for a group than a member simply not showing, giving some lame excuse. For a member to say, 'I wanted to mow the lawn before the rain came', or 'I was feeling too tired to come out' is to communicate a clear message: 'You're just not enough of a priority for me. Other things are simply more important.' The wise leader will not leave it too long before dealing with the issue directly.

Watching the Watch

Nobody likes to be a party-pooper. When the discussion is flowing freely and fruitfully, it's a hard ask to step in and move things on. But if the leader doesn't take responsibility for keeping an eye on time, nobody will. And it matters, because a habitual lack of discipline in this area can easily breed quiet resentment – and so declining morale – among some members.

1. *Leave time to apply*

We've already seen the importance of teasing out good application of the text. But this part of the group's time can easily be consigned to the 'optional', leaving minds, hearts and behaviour unchallenged. Make sure it doesn't go!

2. *Leave time to summarise*

The easiest way to ensure group members forget everything they've learnt within five minutes of walking out the door is to fail to crystallize what has been learnt during the course of the study. Every member, asked next day what the study was about, should readily be able to give a good, accurate and succinct answer.

3. *Leave time to pray*

If it has been a good study, members will be left feeling they have business to do with God. It is right to give an opportunity to begin that business with a prayer time before the meeting's over. So don't forget to build that time into your plan! A good rule of thumb for most groups (where the custom is to share personal prayer requests at this point) might be to set aside around a third of your time for such 'share and prayer', always making sure that what you have learnt in the study informs and shapes how you pray for one another – see the next chapter.

4. *Finish on time*

It might feel super-spiritual to carry on digging into the word of God until late into the night, especially if a number seem to be up for it. But in truth it is usually unloving and may serve to breed irritation among some, whether or not they are open about their feelings. If you've agreed a finish-time, stick to it. You may like to consider renegotiating what time you wind up if most don't seem to be in a hurry to leave. But in general, it's better to leave people wanting more rather than feeling resentful about losing time they had mentally apportioned to something else (e.g. sleep!).

6

Prayer, Care and Personal Nurture

The Emperor Penguin is one tough customer. It has to endure some of the most hostile conditions on earth in the course of its life. Temperatures in the Antarctic winter, its chosen breeding ground, can dip as low as -40° and winds can reach 90 miles per hour. And yet the Emperor Penguin manages to survive, maintaining a constant body temperature higher than that of humans. How does it do it?

In part, it comes down to good design. It has the densest feather coat of any bird alive. Combined with a fairly robust layer of blubber, this makes it a match for some truly dreadful conditions.

But even those fine features won't guarantee its survival when the temperatures really plummet. When the wind bites and the snowstorms blow, the males, whose job it is to incubate the eggs in the breeding season, put into effect a strategy for survival which has served them well. They huddle. Large groups of them stick close together to minimise their exposure to the elements. At any one time, of course, there will be a number of them having a hard time of it out on the edge. But the culture of the group is such that none of them is left out in the cold for long. Before long, one from the 'inside' will come to their aid and take the strain for them. That is how they survive and breed. On their own, few of them would make it. Working together, they keep one another warm and provide relief for their peers exposed to those icy blasts. Those who are relatively toasty have a job to do – to come to the aid of others in need; those being buffeted about by the elements know that it won't be long before relief arrives.

That huddle of penguins is a lovely picture of what a healthy small group might look like, as it shares out the warmth of Christian fellowship. The New Testament is jam-packed with encouragements for how Christian believers might interact with 'one another' in a healthy way. We are to love one another, accept one another, instruct one another, serve one another, carry one another's burdens, be compassionate with one another, teach and admonish one another, encourage one another, spur one another on to love and good deeds, pray for one another – to list but a few! Get your concordance out or fire up your Bible software and you'll see that's just the tip of the iceberg.

Of course, it is the church as a whole for which that pattern of relationships is really laid down. But in practice – as we've already seen – the small group will often be the main context in which those 'one-another' relationships are experienced and lived out. As such, the leader's brief includes an awful lot more than just leading great studies. This chapter looks at three key ways in which groups can – penguin-like – help one another to thrive.

Group Prayer

It's one thing to pray for a spiritual brother or sister. It's quite another to pray *with* them. Any group of believers who love one another and who – when it comes to expressing that love – are prepared to take their cue from their master Jesus will pray for one another. And countless Christians have been lost in wonder as they see the dramatic ways in which God answers such prayers. Missionaries find closed doors opening to them. Sick people see their illness melting away. Those struggling with besetting sins make breakthroughs. God delights to bring his blessings through such intercession.

But when Christian people meet together, they have the opportunity to go a step further: they can pray together. And as they do, they not only express support and encouragement for each other, they have the opportunity to teach godly priorities and to model what mature prayer looks (or rather 'sounds') like.

Have a look at this simple graph.

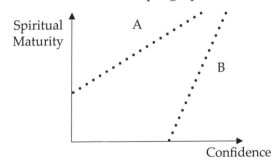

It is quite crude, but it shows two distinct ways in which believers can grow through the corporate prayer life of their small group.

1. Growing in confidence

Some members of your group (type 'A' in the graph) will start from a position of very little confidence when it comes to praying with their spiritual brothers and sisters. They may be secure in their faith and their understanding, serious about living the life of Christian discipleship, and perhaps even disciplined in their personal prayer life. But even the prospect of *open* prayer might throw them into a blind panic. If you are a naturally confident person it might be hard for you to appreciate just how terrifying the thought of contributing to open, extempore prayer could be for these people.

Of course some such people are so naturally timid that – realistically speaking – they are unlikely ever to be able to pray in public. But they are few in number. The great majority of timid pray-ers can learn, through patient and loving guidance, to contribute to the group in this way – to the great encouragement of both themselves and others.

The following diagram provides one possible sequence – or at the very least some ideas – for how to build confidence in group prayer among those who are new to it.

Give the timid member (in advance) a short prayer at the beginning of the study.
A couple of weeks later, invite them to pray in the same 'slot', but in their own words.

Invite the group to come next time with a 1-sentence prayer responding to something they've learnt today, starting 'Thank you, Father, for…'
Next time you meet, invite each member to read out someone else's prayer.

Give the group a few minutes to write down a 1-sentence personal prayer request, giving as an example what you, the leader, are going to write down.
Split into pairs, swap pieces of paper, and suggest each prays for their 'partner' using their words.

Repeat steps 2 and 3, but this time each member is asked to read out his/her own prayer.
They may like to vary the response prayers to begin 'Sorry, Father, for…', or 'Please, Father, help me to…' as well as 'Thank you, Father, for…'

Split into pairs to pray for each other again, but this time ditch the paper and invite prayers more than a sentence long.
Once they're happy praying in pairs, try bigger groups of 3 or 4, and finally remain as a large group.

The process could take only a few meetings, or a whole year. The important thing is to keep trying to go forward. And remember, this is only one possible sequence of steps – do use your imagination and mix things up a bit.

One final thing to say here. Don't be afraid to resort to age-old, tried-and-tested techniques of giving group members confidence to pray. Here are a couple of the best.

- **Pass the cushion**

A cushion is passed around the room during the prayer time. On receiving the cushion, each person knows it is his or her turn to pray, or else remain silent and simply pass it on. The idea is to remove the risk of embarrassing oneself by beginning to pray at the same time as someone else!

- **Put it in the diary**

There are few things more encouraging to a group's prayer life than being able to look back at prayer requests from previous meetings and see ticks added next to them at a later date, signalling the work of God in answer to that prayer. It's a good role for someone to take on – keeper of the prayer diary!

2. *Growing in maturity*

For others, though (type 'B' on the graph), it is not so much lack of confidence but lack of maturity which is the issue. Whether it's because of a naturally confident character, or a good ability with words, an ease with fellow group members or just a familiarity with Christian culture, these people do not struggle to get the words out in this setting. The problem is more about *which* words they get out!

As we've already seen, the small group is a great forum for its members to mature in their personal prayer-lives, that is, to make both the content and the manner of their prayers reflect the Bible's understanding of prayer and therefore what it is our heavenly father wants to hear from us. And as a leader you have a significant opportunity to help this maturing process to happen.

As the diagram shows, there are five particular areas of potential growth to keep in mind as you lead your group.

FROM	TO
Formal	Intimate
Material	Spiritual
Immediate	Eternal
Situations	People
Me-focus	God-focus

- From distance to intimacy

'You did not receive a spirit that makes you a slave again to fear', wrote the apostle Paul in Romans 8:15, 'but you received the Spirit of sonship. And by him we cry "Abba, Father".'

One of the great motivations for Christians to pray is simply that we can! Jesus has done all that is necessary for us to be able to come straight into the presence of our Father God. There's no special formality or formula needed, no special procedures or posture, and no special mode of address or vocabulary. But this is hard to grasp for some. They may need to learn to come into God's presence simply and humbly, speaking to him with the 'naturalness' and intimacy of a child addressing his or her father.

- From the material to the spiritual

There's no denying the invitation of Jesus to pray for 'daily bread' (Matt. 6:11) – that is, material sustenance. But the truth is, much Christian praying doesn't delve any deeper into the Lord's prayer than that one line. Many of us have heard prayers – often from our own lips! – which focus almost exclusively on physical safety, job-hunting, medical procedures, school and university applications, and such things.

While God loves to provide for his children in every way, his greatest concern for us seems to be our progress in Christian character. The fruit of the Spirit is not 'a well-paid job, freedom from illness, and some friends for little Jonny at his new school', but 'love, joy, peace, patience, kindness, goodness, faithfulness, gentleness and self-control' (Gal. 5:22-23). It is these – spiritual – priorities which will inform our prayers as our hearts beat more in time with God's heart.

As our group members grow in maturity, we will find ourselves saying 'Amen' to more and more prayers which ask God to use circumstances to train us in Christian character – even thanking him for allowing us to suffer difficulties which have been the cause of personal growth.

- From the immediate to the eternal

God cares about the present order of things. But neither we ourselves nor the environment in which we live will last for ever. As Christians mature, so they develop an eternal perspective and start to care more about things which will last into the new creation.

In particular, that will mean they will pray less about the healing of the body than the healing of souls. They will develop a love for the lost and a passionate concern for the task of seeing the new creation populated – a concern which far outstrips their concern for the temporary improvement of life in the here and now.

• From situations to people

Christians often pray for opportunities, events, missions, crises, and other situations. But Paul the apostle didn't. He prayed consistently for *people*. 'Since the day we heard about you, we have not stopped praying for *you*...' (Col. 1:9). He was person-focussed in his prayers – and he encouraged others to be like him in this.

As our group members allow the Bible to inform their prayers, we will begin to hear them direct those prayers towards individuals more than situations. They will be asking God to be at work in people (and thanking him for such work apparently already done) – perhaps *in* and *through* situations, but never losing sight of the people themselves as the primary objects of God's concern.

• From 'me-focus' to 'God-focus'

We've all heard it; we've all given it. It's the prayer shopping list. The catalogue of things we'd like from God or of ways in which we'd like him to intervene in our lives for our benefit.

As we've already seen, God is not averse to hearing our requests. On the contrary, 'In everything, by prayer and petition, with thanksgiving', wrote Paul, 'present your requests to God' (Phil. 4:6).

But remember the first priority Jesus taught us to express in our prayers: 'Hallowed be your name'. It is God's name, his reputation, his glory, which is to be uppermost in the prayer-life of his disciples. Think of the way that Paul so often frames his prayers, or indeed his great interjections (e.g. Eph. 3:20-21 and 1 Tim. 1:17).

Once again, as group members grow in 'prayer-maturity', they will likely be lining up to adore God for who he is, to revel in his greatness and seek the glory of his name, before mentioning their own more personal concerns – or at least as the motivation for God's meeting such concerns.

The group leader will want to be serious and deliberate about facilitating these five dimensions of growth in prayer-maturity among the group. But how? Here are a few suggestions.

➤ Work at it!

As always in Christian ministry, the work starts in our own hearts. The leader needs to be committed to growing in his or her own prayer-maturity.

➤ Model it!

There's an old Christian chorus: 'They are watching you, marking all you do, hearing the things you say...' It's true in a small group. Over time, the members will learn to prioritise what the leader prioritises.

➤ Teach it!

There's no harm in being explicit about what prayer-maturity looks like. Consider, for example, asking one willing member per meeting to share what they've gleaned from studying one of the prayers of the Bible during the week – or do it yourself!

➤ Commend it!

When you hear signs of godly priorities in people's prayers, say so! Consider a word in their ear as they leave the meeting, or a text or email shortly afterwards, to say what encouraged you about their prayer.

➤ Schedule it!

Think about the structure of your meeting. Some groups schedule personal prayer concerns for the beginning of the meeting (to make it easier to focus on God's concerns afterwards). Others leave them to the end (to encourage 'from-the-passage prayer' first of all and so take a steer from the Bible's priorities). Some even feel the need to have an occasional 'medical-free' prayer time! What would work best for your group?

➤ Wait for it!

The culture of a group can take a while to change, so do be patient and don't lose heart if the group's prayer-life doesn't seem to be moving on. Reorienting the desires of people's hearts requires a work of the Spirit – so keep praying for this work as you wait.

Caring for Group Members

Many churches and Christian organisations see their small group network as the first line of individual care. And with good reason. The self-disclosure which is required for personal needs and issues to be addressed needs an atmosphere of trust, a context of recognised support, a place of safety. These are all things which are the strong suit of a healthy small group. So how can we capitalise on the opportunities here?

1. Getting to the issue

We're all different when it comes to how comfortable we are, sharing at a deep level with others. There is a whole spectrum from 'Heart-on-the-sleeve Harry' to 'No-comment-Norah'. And this does need to be recognised. For some, divulging matters of the heart is second nature and – if anything – they are just *too* ready to share; for others of a more private disposition, to share even what might seem a relatively superficial morsel of personal information requires an act of immense courage and trust. How can we make our small group a forum where even 'No-comment-Norah' feels able to let others into her life?

- **Set the tone**
  As a group leader, there are a number of traits you may need to cultivate – explicitly or implicitly – in the dynamic of the group if you are to embolden

the more reticent group members to the point where they feel comfortable sharing.

One is an atmosphere of **loving care and good will** towards one another as individuals. There are any number of ways of assuring members how much they are valued. These range from the simple and practical (e.g. remembering their birthday, anniversary and other 'life events', the follow-up phone call after they miss a meeting, flowers when they're ill) to the more costly and involved (praying for them daily and making sure they know you are, stepping in to take care of practicalities like meals and child-care at times of personal or family crisis, helping them move or paint their new house).

Such things can often send a message out of all proportion to the effort involved: he or she knows that you care, that you're on their side.

A second trait worth cultivating in the group is that of **mutual acceptance and non-judgmentalism**. There is a tricky balancing act involved here. On the one hand, as Christian brothers and sisters, we want to hold each other up to the mark, to 'stir up one another towards love and good works' (Heb. 10:24 esv). We need a degree of accountability towards one another, to be shown our sin and have the bar raised for us, to recalibrate our consciences. On the other hand, we need to know that we're accepted as fellow sinners, fellow travellers on the journey of faith, that we'll be treated gently, warmly and with understanding.

One final and vital trait that's needed to provide a feeling of 'safety' is that of **confidentiality**. Whether or not confidentiality is specifically requested on a given matter, the ground-rules of keeping things within the four walls of the group must be applied on matters which are clearly highly personal. It may take regular reminders of this operating principle and a good history of seeing that people do indeed abide by it before some will open up. Absolute confidentiality is not always possible (e.g. criminal activities must by law be reported), but a healthy group will have a zero-tolerance policy towards talking out of turn.

There is one more thing to be aware of here. There can be a great degree of guilt and self-re-crimination in those who find it hard to share: 'Why am I so completely incapable of expressing myself like everyone else?' Alongside any encouragement to speak up, these more private people need to hear that it's OK to keep their counsel. They need to be given time and space to 'warm up' towards personal sharing.

- Set the limits

When the conversation in a small group begins to flow freely in matters beyond the trivial and superficial, a quantum leap takes place. There is an ease that marks the relationships and the group dynamic, which can feel exhilarating and liberating. People express it differently. The small group can be a 'haven', a 'family', a 'rock'.

But just talking is not enough. The New Testament is full of exhortations to self-control, or 'taming the tongue' as James puts it (James 3). In other words, in any given context, including a small group, there are some things which simply ought not to be said. Here are three questions that any group member could be encouraged to consider from time to time.

Question 1: 'Am I being dishonest?'

It is all too easy, as we all know, to lapse into exaggeration, to paint ourselves in a whiter shade than the reality, to present a half-truth as the whole truth, or – more subtly – to express mere opinion as though it were incontrovertible truth. But all of these are simply different ways of being dishonest. If such lapses are not checked, eventually group members will pick up on them and begin to take things that an individual says with a large pinch of salt. This can of course be catastrophic. Quite apart from tolerating what the Bible roundly condemns (e.g. Eph. 4:25), it can lead, like the boy who cried wolf or the faulty smoke detector that's always going off, to situations of real gravity being shrugged off as false alarms.

Question 2: 'Am I being inappropriate?'

There are some things which while true and very personal, are simply not appropriate to share in a group setting. Whether it is something about the past or something very much in the present, it is probably not appropriate to talk about struggles in the area of sexuality, for example, in a mixed group. Similarly there may be deep sensitivities within the group on subjects such as infertility, singleness, or even unemployment which may make some kinds of sharing unkind or inappropriate in some other way. As a leader you would be wise to step in and invite the person sharing to chat with you on an individual basis.

Question 3: 'Am I being a gossip?'
It is all too easy to abuse the safety and the 'sharing' ethos offered by a small group as a means to spread information about other people known to fellow group members. The motivation – whether acknowledged or not – is often to recruit support in a dispute of some kind, to protect personal interests, to slander another as a form of revenge, or simply to develop a reputation as one who holds information. Paul condemns gossips in the same breath as murderers and God-haters (Rom. 1:29-30), and we must take our cue from him. Those who indulge in this way need to be helped gently to see exactly what they are doing and encouraged to avoid it.

• Set the pace
We have been discussing how to create an environment where members of the group feel able to disclose personal needs and struggles, and can be encouraged to do so within certain boundaries. In all this, though, the one who

will make the most difference is likely to be the group leader. As you make yourself vulnerable to the group through your own (appropriate) self-disclosure, you will be issuing the most powerful invitation to others to do the same. Try to let people into your life. Share your thinking in your decisions. Speak about your struggles. Ask for advice. Be open about ways in which you'd love to see God change you. And keep doing this: every time you do, you will be chipping away at the defences around some in the group.

2. Understanding the issue

It may be something they said in passing during the Bible study. It may be something that was mentioned during the prayer time. Or it may be something that you've picked up privately – the conversation in the kitchen while making coffee, or when the two of you were the last to leave or the first to arrive. In whatever context you learned of the issue, you know about it now, and it's real and active for the individual.

As a leader, or as co-leaders in a group, it is important to keep up with those in your care: a diligent leader will make sure each member meets with one of the leaders in the group one-to-one, at least three or four times a year. In the context of such meetings, you are bound to become aware from time to time of personal needs and issues in the life of those in your care.

It may on occasion be appropriate to explore the issue as a whole group. More often it will be easier to talk about it in a personal conversation outside group time (even if something has been shared with the group at large, you may want to follow it up one-to-one later). But where do you start?

Lack of information can be a dangerous thing. Your willingness to help may completely backfire if you don't have a good understanding of the situation. The place to begin, then, is heartfelt prayer for wisdom and insight and then a gentle teasing out – through active listening – of exactly what is going on.

Quite often the act of listening itself is all the help that is needed. In helping the person simply to articulate the issue, you will be equipping them to solve it. But good listening does not come naturally to many of us; it is a demanding thing which involves considerable emotional and intellectual (and sometimes physical!) energy. But even though it may not come naturally, good listening skills can be learnt. Here are a few tips to get you started

- **Use your heart**

  Good listening begins not with the ears, but with the heart. It comes from placing a high value on the individual. It comes from loving them. Those with a problem-solving mentality need to learn to focus on the person rather than the problem. If you really love them, you will find it easier to understand them, because your concern will outweigh your tiredness, your distractions, and your self-interest. More than that, they will know. They will see it for themselves, because it will be real and evident in your face, your body language, and perhaps even your tears. They will find it easier to open up to you because they are convinced of one thing: 'This person really cares about me'.

• Use your imagination

Empathy is at heart an exercise in imagination. To understand how somebody is feeling – and why – requires the imaginative act of thinking ourselves into their situation. 'What would it feel like if *my* parents spoke to *me* like that?' This imaginative act allows us to engage well and suggest to the person ways of articulating what they are feeling: 'You must have felt so undermined!' etc.

• Use your eyes

Researchers estimate that only 7 per cent of communication involves actual words, 38 per cent is vocal (i.e. through the pitch, speed, volume and tone of the voice), but a whopping 55 per cent of it is visual: it is a matter of body language and eye contact.

If they are right, then we need to train ourselves to learn from our eyes as much as we learn from our ears – if not more! Those who are skilled at doing this will often attest that it can be much more reliable than words. But don't forget what they can see in you too. Do use your body language and eye contact to reassure, to affirm, and to express loving concern. The nod, the smile, and the leaning forward may feel clichéd and unnatural, but they all communicate something important: 'I'm interested. I care.'

- **Use your tongue**

Good listening involves good speaking. You may
need to help the person simply to get started, or
to keep going at a pause: 'So how did it start?',
'Where did that leave you?' You may need to
take things down a level from events to personal
reactions: 'How did that impact you?', 'You must
have been furious!' Or you may need to clarify or
confirm what has been said: 'Sorry, just to be clear,
what exactly was it that made you feel that way?',
'So what I hear you saying is...'

In all this, you are simply trying to diagnose the issue.
You are listening, trying to understand where they are.

3. Helping with the issue

One of the first questions we naturally ask ourselves once
somebody has confided their struggles in us is: 'How can
I help?' But this may be a difficult question to answer. It may
need to be broken down into a series of further questions.

- **How do they *want* to be helped?**

This is perhaps the easiest question, and can often
be resolved by a direct enquiry: 'What can I do?' It
may be that all they really wanted you to do was to
listen to them, to love them, to reassure them and
perhaps to pray for them or with them. But they
may have something else in mind: clear advice for
a tricky situation, some specific practical help.

Whatever it is, you may need to push a little to
confirm there is nothing more. Embarrassment,
or a worry about putting you or others out, may
make it difficult to articulate what they're really

hoping for. Or their state of mind may be such that they need even the most basic decisions being made for them. You may need to make suggestions, or even insistences: 'Would it help if I ...?', 'Is there something practical we could do, for example ...?', 'I'm going to pick you up tomorrow and take you to ...'.

• **How do they *need* to be helped?**
The person in difficulty is not always the best judge of what they really need. But this is where we feel the benefit of being part of God's household. A fresh pair of eyes, an outside perspective, and a more objective approach can be a great boon. This is the business of professional consultants of all shapes and sizes. But it is also the business of Christians. Hence Paul's frequent instructions to step in to one another's lives: 'We urge you brothers, warn those who are idle, encourage the timid, help the weak, be patient with everyone. Make sure that nobody pays back evil for evil ...' (1 Thess. 5:14-15).

Armed with God's Scriptures ('useful for teaching, rebuking, correcting, and training in righteousness ...', 2 Tim. 3:16), God's Spirit ('The spiritual man makes judgments about all things ...', 1 Cor. 2:15) and God's good sense ('If any of you lacks wisdom, he should ask God...', James 1:5), we can discern what it is that is really required.

It may be some practical love (somebody to look after the kids, or to provide a lift). Or it could be friendship, somebody to walk closely with them for a period. Maybe some guidance is what's needed – a good, biblical steer. Perhaps even a challenge or rebuke, even if what they were hoping for was affirmation.

• **How far can they be helped by me?**

It is an essential skill of any would-be helper to know their limits. If we try to help beyond our level of understanding and skill, we can do more damage than good. Sometimes we will need to turn to the police (if we learn of a crime). Sometimes it will be a professional counsellor we turn to, or a pastor or somebody who has gone through a similar experience. Sometimes we may find ideas on how to help in a book or an online resource. But wherever we need to look, the mindset must always be: 'How can I best serve my Christian brother or sister?'

We may find ourselves faced with questions of sexuality, depression, the after-effects of an abusive background, eating disorders, self-harm or other psychological disorders. These things may make us feel uncomfortable or worse. In such cases we would be well-advised to seek permission to involve outside help. Certainly we will need to be alert to the danger of forging a demanding and dependent relationship which we cannot sustain. All that said, there is a great deal to be said for simply expressing love and support, giving godly guidance and practical help in conjunction with those close to them, and encouraging them in their walk with God.

• How far can they be helped by the group?
Combining forces to help out a fellow member of the small group who's in a tough spot is not only good for that individual. It's good for the group. There are few things which can bond a group together as strongly as a shared work of practical service.

Why not form a babysitting rota among you for the couple whose marriage is under strain so that they can get out and spend time together on a regular basis? Or make sure between you that the hospitalised group member has at least one visitor a day? Or form a working party to help a member move house? Or work together to organise a birthday party for a member who is feeling isolated from friends and family?

There may be a need to protect some in the group from feeling pressured into helping, when in fact their own circumstances are somewhat fragile. But it is a wonderful group-building thing to look after one another in this way, as well as a powerful witness to the outside world of the love which binds Christian believers together.

Nurturing Individuals
It was 12.55 p.m. on Thursday. Time to be off. Each and every week, for the best part of a year, I would jump on

my bike at that time, head over to my friend's place and be greeted warmly five minutes later. A good lunch awaited us at the canteen where he ate every day – and even better, it was on him. As an older member of a Christian group I belonged to, he saw these meetings as an integral part of his ministry.

We'd catch up on this and that, make appreciative comments about the apple pie and custard, and then head to his room just around the corner. On would go the kettle, and five minutes later, we'd be sitting down with a mug in one hand and a Bible in the other, with him helping me come to grips with the meaning and application of the passage in front of us. Often we'd be right off the subject within another five minutes, tackling an issue of my own Christian life that had only the most superficial bearing on the text before us. There'd be no ducking it: he'd patiently and wisely help me think through the issue. He'd listen to my concerns, share his own experiences, leave me with some big questions to mull over. But somehow we'd find our heads back in the text before too long, slowly putting the pieces of the jigsaw puzzle together in my young and very incomplete understanding of the Christian faith.

I'd be back at my place shortly after 2 p.m. – the whole excursion would have lasted little more than an hour. But when it comes to shaping my understanding of the Christian faith and working out priorities for my Christian life, that series of one-to-one meetings was probably the most formative experience of my life. Such is the power of one-to-one ministry.

As a small group leader, you will likely have both the experience and the credibility to nurture individual members of your group in their personal discipleship through meeting one-to-one with them. The initiative for meeting might come from them or from you. The meeting might be on a *one-off* or *ad hoc* basis – perhaps exploring in more depth an issue they struggled with in the context of the small group but which was impossible or inappropriate to deal with there. Or it could develop into a *regular* meeting where you agree a plan or project to work at together.

1. What to do together

What might such a project be? Anything that will mature the faith of the group member! Well-trodden paths in this regard include:

- Studying a book of the Bible.

Choose one appropriate to where he or she is: e.g. take a gospel (or selected passages from one) for a non-Christian; one of the shorter letters of Paul (Philippians or Colossians are favourites) for a young Christian; one of the pastorals (e.g. 1 Tim. or 2 Tim.) for somebody wanting to go further in Christian ministry; or simply a book that he or she would love to get a handle on or that you feel you know well enough to be able to act as a reliable guide.

- Reading a Christian book.

You might choose one that addresses a specific Bible doctrine (e.g. the cross or the Christian hope); or a particular issue of significance to your group member (e.g. medical ethics or prayer); or a particular area of practical ministry skill (e.g. how to lead a music ministry or lead a Bible-study group). Alternatively it could be an area in which interest was triggered by something said at one of your group meetings: predestination, perhaps, or the Holy Spirit. Many Christian books include questions at the end of each chapter which may help your discussion time together.

• Setting your own programme.

It may be that your group member is keen to be more effective in personal evangelism, but is stumped by the questions people throw back. Why not make a list of the seven most often asked questions or objections to the Christian faith and each time you meet discuss some of the approaches you might take with somebody held back by one of those questions. Maybe he or she is struggling with maintaining a lively personal prayer life. You could make a list together of some of the great prayers of the Bible and look at them one by one, noting their priorities and discussing how they might shape the prayer-life of a twenty-first century disciple.

These are just a few suggestions for *what* you might do. The key thing to be clear on, though, is the *why*.

2. *Why spend the time nurturing individuals?*

Why commit such time and energy to such a seemingly inefficient work as nurturing one or more members of your small group as individuals?

On one level, the answer is the same as that for any form of Christian ministry. In Paul's words, 'We proclaim him, admonishing and teaching everyone with all wisdom, so that we may present everyone perfect in Christ' (Col. 1:28). We want to bring people to perfection (i.e. maturity) in Christ.

But one-to-one ministry (or personal work, mentoring, discipling or reading with individuals, as it is variously known) is a particularly effective way of achieving this. The route to Christian maturity is, says Paul, through a deliberate putting to death of what belongs to the earthly nature (Col. 3:5) and – having stripped off the 'old self with its practices' – getting dressed in the 'new self, which is being renewed in knowledge in the image of its Creator' (Col. 3:9-10).

Putting to death can of course be done by indiscriminate machine-gun fire. But how much more effective to adopt the careful approach of a sniper. Providing new clothes can be done by emptying a pallet-full of random-sized clothing onto a crowd of people and waiting to see what happens. But surely the results would be better if we were to send a tailor to each person in turn, measuring them up and making clothes to fit.

So it is with the work of nurturing individuals in our care. It gives the opportunity to scratch where it itches, to fill up where the gap is, and to teach and train according to the capacity, gifts, blindspots and passions of the individual.

3. How to go about it

Before you start meeting, there are just a few guidelines to bear in mind.

- **Choose wisely – but don't be too picky!**

How do you decide who to invest time and energy in? A basic rule of thumb is: 'feed the hungry'. Where you see an appetite for growth, or for increasing in understanding, your efforts are unlikely to be wasted. Clearly there will be some people whom you are less suited to meeting with personally. It is rarely appropriate for a leader to meet regularly with somebody of the opposite sex – unless he or she is old enough to be your grandparent! But also be wary of spending time with a married person whose spouse is likely to be less than supportive of the arrangement. Be wise. That said, don't wait until the perfect person comes into the frame – you could be waiting a long time!

- **Start slowly – but keep the pressure on!**

Rather than going straight in with all guns blazing, outlining your plan for weekly meetings over the next year (which might be seen as a little on the 'heavy' side), consider teeing up a one-off meeting, in a comfortable and relaxed environment, to talk through some issue. Maybe organise a follow-up meeting if there's anything either of you needs to go away and think through. At that second meeting, take the temperature and if you feel the invitation would be received warmly, suggest the idea of meeting up regularly.

- **Have a plan – but sit lightly to it**

Unless you have a 'project' to get stuck into together, your meetings are likely to peter out or at least prove not particularly productive. Enthusiasm will only get you so far; discipline has to come into the picture at some stage. It is generally helpful to have a clear agenda for your meetings (e.g. a project like those mentioned above). But don't feel the need to follow this slavishly. If a real issue has come up since you last met, don't worry about giving over half your time – or even *all* your time – to talking this through. Departing from the 'plan' like this may be difficult if you've prepared carefully for your meeting, or you are a fairly structured person by nature, but that unplanned conversation may prove the most helpful and fruitful time you've ever had!

- Share your life - but avoid guru status!

By forming a deliberate nurturing relationship, you will have a wonderful and natural opportunity to open a window into your life and thinking. This can be very powerful – often young Christians long to see what discipleship 'looks like' in real life, at least as much as talking about it in theory. And don't worry about sharing failures and weaknesses as well as successes – as long as you show you're serious about repentance and growth yourself, you'll give weight to your ministry. Just be aware of what your status is becoming. It's fine to be a spiritual father or mother; not so good to become a guru.

- Spot the gaps, but remember grace!

As you get to know one another better, you will begin to spot areas of your group member's lifestyle which fall short of the Bible's ideal. It may be in their attitude to money and possessions, work and career, sex and relationships, drink and leisure – or some other area. The issues may come up spontaneously, or they may need to be gently teased out. Do take the opportunity to hold him or her to account; you might consider asking to be held to account yourself. But remember we are all sinners who fail in different areas: let your rebuke be gentle and grace-filled, thoroughly tinged with the assurance of forgiveness.

- **Work hard – but play hard too!**

Finally, however serious you are in your work together, do remember that your influence as a nurturer will be strengthened if you are able to spend occasional leisure time together. Go for a walk or cycle ride, catch a movie or a concert, or at least have a meal with no agenda once in a while!

Appendix 1

Evaluating the Study

One of the best resources available to you to help you lead better Bible studies is your co-leader (if you have one). By providing guidance and feedback to one another as a 'critical friend', you will help one another to spot areas which need more work.

But it is possible to do better than a simple 'How did I do?' The chart overleaf provides a framework for structured feedback covering a number of key areas which would benefit from appraisal. Used well, and in the context of good will and encouragement, it should help you to be sharpened and made more effective in your role.

You can use the chart in different ways. You may simply wish to run through the different categories as a 'grid' for verbal feedback. But once in a while it may be helpful to fill it in and give to your co-leader to take away. To make this easier, you may wish to photocopy and enlarge the chart to provide sufficient space for your comments.

One thing: don't be put off by the score column! It's just a useful indicator for the leader to see quickly and clearly which bits he or she is doing well and which aspects could do with some work.

Area	Score	Comment
Key points *How faithful to the passage were the key points communicated during the study?*		
Use of time *How well did the discussion time reflect the relative importance of the various points?*		
Observation *How effectively & creatively did the leader help the group to observe what the text said?*		
Interpretation *How successfully did the leader help the group to understand what the text meant?*		
Application *How well did the leaders help the group to apply the text to understanding, attitude and life?*		
Dynamic *How appropriate was the balance of contributions (member-member and members-leader)?*		
Follow-up *How well did the leader tease out and probe members' answers? How flexible was the study plan?*		
Practicalities *How smoothly did the evening go? To what extent were possible distractions dealt with properly?*		

Appendix 2

A Sample Covenant

Many groups find it helpful to clarify the aims and modus operandi of the group. The process is often the most important thing here – so consider spending a good amount of time on it. You'll probably want to cover aims, attendance, ethos, timings, and roles – as well as possibly other areas.

You may end up with something like the example below – but remember: make it your own. This is only one possibility of the shape of such a document!

As members of the Bible Study group led by Jack and Roseanne Spufford, we agree to work together to build each other up towards maturity in Christ. To that end we will

1. Make a real priority of our meetings, save for illness, unavoidable work commitments or holidays. If we cannot make it, we will contact Jack or Roseanne explaining why. We will be punctual, arriving in time for us to begin by 8:15 p.m.

2. Treat one another with respect, as brothers and sisters. We will honour confidences, put one another's needs above our own, support each other in prayer and allow each other time to contribute. We will aim to become vulnerable to one another, sharing freely and openly.

3. We will aim to spend at least one hour in Bible study and at least twenty minutes in prayer, as well as any time for talking and mutual encouragement.

4. We will each play our part in the life of the group. Jack and Roseanne will do most of the leading. Bob and Christine will normally host. Tim will organise refreshments. Lucy will keep the prayer diary. Steve and Jemima will act as social secretary. And Ian will co-ordinate emails and other communications.

Signed

....
....
....
....
....
....
....
....

Date: 8 May 2010

Appendix 3

Resources

Leading a small group, like any Christian ministry, involves hard work. It did for Paul: 'For this I toil, struggling with all his energy that he powerfully works within me' (Col. 1:29 ESV). And it must for us. Part of that work inevitably includes equipping ourselves to do things to serve better. Here are some ideas of where to go from here as you think through the material covered in this book.

Preparing for Leadership

James Lawrence, *Growing Leaders* (CPAS, 2004)
Derek Tidball, *Skilful Shepherds* (Apollos, 1996)

Managing the Group

Steve & Mandy Briars, *Homegroups: The Authentic Guide* (Authentic Lifestyle, 2006)
Neal McBride, *How to Lead Small Groups* (NavPress, 1990)

Mapping Out the Study and Leading

Rod & Karen Morris, *Leading Better Bible Studies* (Aquila, 1997)
Colin Marshall, *Growth Groups* (London: St Matthias Press, 1996)

Prayer, Care and Personal Nurture

Ronald Dunn, *Don't Just Stand There, Pray Something!* (Zondervan, 2001)

Peter Hicks, *What Could I Say: A Handbook for Helpers* (IVP, 2000)

Sophie Peace, *One-to-One: A Discipleship Handbook* (Authentic Lifestyle, 2003)

Here are some titles ideal for small group studies ...

READ / MARK / LEARN Series

Read / Mark / Learn is a small group Bible study series that is designed to equip people to study God's Word for themselves - and in studying it, know God's purpose for their lives.

Each book studies whole books of the Bible and so enables people to understand scripture in context. In an era that claims that the Bible can say what you want it to say it is important to re-establish the truth that you just can't - if you explain the scripture with honesty, fairness and in context. Each Study establishes:

- the context, aim and structure of the passage.
- links with the Old Testament
- lessons from each part of the passage – highlighting key issues
- practical applications and suggestions

Each section also includes conversational discussion starters and suggested questions for leading a Bible study. There is also a section for photocopying for group members to pre-prepare for each study

Read / Mark / Learn has been established for over 30 years and has proved, internationally, to be a successful way to hold satisfying and enjoyable group Bible studies. It has been developed by one of London's leading churches, St Helens, Bishopsgate.

Books of the Bible in the Series:

Romans (ISBN 978-1-84550-3-628)
John (ISBN 978-1-84550-3-611)

Christian Focus Publications

publishes books for all ages

Our mission statement –
STAYING FAITHFUL
In dependence upon God we seek to impact the world through literature faithful to His infallible Word, the Bible. Our aim is to ensure that the Lord Jesus Christ is presented as the only hope to obtain forgiveness of sin, live a useful life and look forward to heaven with Him.

REACHING OUT
Christ's last command requires us to reach out to our world with His gospel. We seek to help fulfill that by publishing books that point people towards Jesus and help them develop a Christ-like maturity. We aim to equip all levels of readers for life, work, ministry and mission.

Books in our adult range are published in three imprints.

Christian Focus contains popular works including biographies, commentaries, basic doctrine and Christian living. Our children's books are also published in this imprint.

Mentor focuses on books written at a level suitable for Bible College and seminary students, pastors, and other serious readers. The imprint includes commentaries, doctrinal studies, examination of current issues and church history.

Christian Heritage contains classic writings from the past.

Christian Focus Publications, Ltd
Geanies House, Fearn, Ross-shire,
IV20 1TW, Scotland, United Kingdom
info@christianfocus.com
www.christianfocus.com